Pathetically Apathetic

HARLEY LIECHTY

Credits

Author: Harley Liechty
Illustrator: Mariah Anthony

Proof Readers:

- Robert Redmond
- Jon Kelly
- Sydnee Hollingsworth
- Samuel Greer
- Danielle Simms
- Maia Cruse
- Adrian Hernandez

Proof Editor: Samuel Greer, Jon Kelly
Type-Editor & Book Designer: Clay Clark Publishing
Emotional Supporter: Danielle Simms

Dedication

This book was written for myself, so that I might live a great, intentional life, in the labor I want to work in. It's also written to those who seek to intentionally build a great life for themselves.

What Other Readers Thought About *Pathetically Apathetic*

*"It's an ironic endeavor you've undertaken, **trying to provoke passion into your openly dispassionate audience.**"*

*"I loved it a lot. I feel like there was a lot of revealing how the 'average' lifestyle is so apathetic. **I felt called out, but in a good way!**"*

*"I pick up three voices in your writing. The voice of research and its demonstration. The voice of questioning it. Your internal voice tying loose ends. **I enjoy your writing!**"*

*"I think it's bold. Daring. **It doesn't shy away from hard truths, but still has moments that bring you back with grace and patience that is needed for the process**. I am really enjoying it! It's challenging some ideas and things I've been struggling with in my personal life so I think it will do that for others as well."*

*"It's a tell ya straight kind of book that challenges the reader to evaluate their actions and motives to become a non-apathetic, intentional and driven individual. **This would be a book I could frequently come back to**. Even though this topic could become heavy and depressing, it doesn't feel that way reading it because of the use of life examples, practical action plans and real-talk."*

CONTENTS

Chapter 1: Solving Problems 101 - It's Simple, But Difficult for Most 19

Chapter 2: Most Don't Care (The Undeniable Reality) 33

Chapter 3: Trust: The First Dysfunction 53

Chapter 4: The Enormous Problem With Saving the World 77

Chapter 5: Obsession is Weird 95

Chapter 6: Environment & the Mentorship 117

Chapter 7: Apathetic vs. Non-Apathetic: A Case Study 143

Chapter 8: Most Will Not Follow Your Lead 161

Chapter 9: But, Wait...Do You Really? 169

Chapter 10: "Be Fruitful, Then Multiply." 193

Chapter 11: Daily Planning and Time Blocking 201

Chapter 12: What Will You Be Satisfied With? 215

Chapter 13: Stop Waiting for the Right Moment 231

Pathetically Apathetic

Copyright © 2020 by Clay Clark Publishing

Published by Clay Clark Publishing 1100 Suite #100 Riverwalk Terrace

Jenks, OK 74037

Printed in the United States of America. All rights reserved, because we think ahead. Not a single part of this book may be copied or reproduced in any manner without the express written consent of the National Football League which will never actually give you consent because they are in no way, shape or form associated with the creation of this book. For additional information, address Clay Clark Publishing or a guy named "Smith" at 1100 Riverwalk Terrace #1100, Jenks, OK, 74037.

Additional books can be purchased for educational, business or sales promotional use. For more information, please email the Special Markets Department at info@ThrivetimeShow.com or the author directly at harley.liechty@gmail.com.

Pathetically Apathetic

An Introduction to Apathy

I might as well jump to the question you're already thinking: **what's so important or different about THIS book?** What makes this one stand out in the crowd of other helpful books? Who the heck is this "Harley" guy? I would be asking the same questions if I were you.

Unlike the motivational speakers, business tycoons or celebrities that typically write helpful books, I have no obvious reason for writing a self-help book. I grew up as a privileged white kid in Dallas, Texas, with all of my needs easily met. There were no worries of making the mortgage or car payments. There were no teenage pregnancies or jail sentences. I wasn't born with a disability or limp. I don't have a dramatic story that could be told onstage to motivate a roaring crowd.

So, why the heck did I write this book? Because really, there are plenty of helpful books out there. There are a lot of smart people who earned PHDs, built great businesses and persevered through terrible times. Because of their great triumphs, they want to share their knowledge. They sit down for interviews to share their life stories. They write books to inspire us. They create curriculums we can pay for so they can share the "really good stuff."

Most of these smart people have good intentions with their work. They want to improve the world. It makes them sad that so few people share in their wealth. So, year after year, there's always a new book to help teach the "hidden secrets" to success.

The thing is, I don't have any secrets to give you. There aren't any hidden revelations or treasures to discover in this book. Not to burst any bubbles here, but all those secrets the other books talk about? Yeah, those aren't really secrets. That's just a nice phrase to convince you of the author's guru-esque knowledge. The real truth is, **I can't promise that your life will dramatically change for the better because of this book.**

That being said, this book *could* be absolutely fascinating to you. It *could* be one of your favorite books you've ever read. It *could* mess with your ideas on life and positively impact you. It did with some of my test readers before publishing. What I look to illustrate in this book is a clear, honest understanding about a core truth with our society. Here's the deal: **most people are apathetic.**

It's more than just not caring about some kid in Africa. It's an apathy that's deep within our society and accepted by everyone. There's a cognitive dissonance, a conflict within ourselves, that we all suffer from. We keep coming up with great ideas for our future, but these ideas and ambitions always seem to fall short, without us really knowing why. That's what cognitive dissonance is, thoughts not lining up with actions. **No matter how much knowledge is available to us, we fail to make positive actions a reality in our lives.**

If you've read a lot of books on personal development, but you just can't seem to find a breakthrough, this *could* be your book. If you like getting bold, honest feedback about how the world works, this is definitely your book. **If you like a book with practical, actionable steps to actually solve your problems, you can walk away from this book with clarity.**

While I'm not a guy who's earned a PHD, persevered through dramatic injuries or pulled myself out of immense poverty, I did do one thing: **I changed from being an apathetic person to a caring, non-apathetic person.** I examined my life and realized that I didn't know how to genuinely improve myself. **I didn't know HOW to take**

action. HOW do I become a guy who actually sees things through to the end?

For the past three years, since I was 22 years old, I started to get honest with myself. I took action. I failed to honor my actions plenty of times. But, because of these past three years, I can now confidently move forward towards whatever desires I have in my heart. **I've proven to myself that I can actually turn desire into reality.** I'll be using many stories, quotes, studies and statistics to back myself up, but I can't deny that, at 25 years old, the rest of my life looks pretty exciting.

If you need a book like this, prepare yourself. While this book can bring you the positive results I've experienced, those results come with pain and honesty. I'll look to challenge you on the many assumptions we all face about ourselves and about life. **We're all part of this issue. We're all quite apathetic, and it's about time you learned why.**

· · · ·

Speaking of challenges, I'll go ahead and start with one of the core assumptions in our culture. Psychologists have studied this topic extensively and it's deeply ingrained in our society. It unites us, for better or for worse.

Do You Believe You're a Good Person?

Most people believe they are. Luke Bryan, the country singer, even sang about this in his song, "Most People Are Good," which topped the U.S. & Canadian Billboard Country charts in 2017. In research conducted by Patrick Heck, a social psychologist, he finds that 65% of Americans believe they are above average in intelligence, which I'd say is a good character trait. Whether it's because of our morals, past accomplishments or our social status, we consider ourselves to be really awesome people.

Do I believe I'm a good person? Well, let's run through a list of "good things" about me. I'm not a smoker. I don't shoplift. I don't have a gambling problem, shop irresponsibly, and I'm also not overweight. I work at a business consulting firm, which I'd say is a slightly cooler job than working at a gas station. I don't think I'm a giant loser...so yeah, I think those are some good reasons, right?

Research tells a different, deeper story.

According to a 2016 journal titled, *The Illusion of Moral Superiority*," psychologists from the University of London concluded that, ***"virtually all individuals irrationally inflated their moral qualities."*** This study gathered 265 people online to fill out various questions regarding 30 character traits. These character traits dealt with topics like morality, agency and sociability. Participants were asked to rate themselves and other people on these specific character traits. The objective of the study was to test the "irrational" factor for people's self-belief in their moral superiority.

The results of the study determined that, ***"While it's widely regarded that people grant themselves as 'morally superior' over others, it's highly irrational."*** Here's how they discuss this:

Pathetically Apathetic

*"The irrationality of moral superiority was borne out of the ubiquity of virtue—**almost everyone reported a strong positive moral self-image**—and individuals' ignorance of this ubiquity when making judgments of the average person. Indeed, **neglecting the prototypicality of one's own self-judgments may signal an error in inductive reasoning.**"*

For average people like myself who needed to Google words like "ubiquity" or "prototypicality", the researchers concluded an error in our human reasoning. **Everyone individually believes they're higher and mightier than everyone else.**

You can find numerous studies about how people view themselves as better than others. Psychologists will use terms like, **"illusory superiority."** This is, essentially, **a cognitive bias where we overestimate the quality of our own abilities.** *The Bias Blindspot* research article, conducted by Stanford University, revealed that *"people rate themselves as less subject to various biases than the average American."* These same researchers did follow-up studies with the participants. In the second and third rounds, they educated them with articles and other studies about how people are affected by self-bias, hoping to educate them in their erroneous ways. **Even still, the same participants doubled-down on their claims of not being affected by self-biases.** They boldly claimed these numerous studies didn't apply to them.

Another research journal article titled, *Flawed Self-Assessment: Implications for Health, Education, and the Workplace,* described observations regarding how participants assessed themselves and their individual health. Let's see what they concluded.

An Introduction to Apathy

> ***"People are unrealistically optimistic about their own health risks compared with those of other people.*** *Guided by mistaken but seemingly plausible theories of health and disease, people misdiagnose themselves—a phenomenon that can have severe consequences for their health and longevity."*

Here's what the same journal had to say about these implications with education:

> *"Research in education finds that students' assessments of their performance tend to agree only moderately with those of their teachers and mentors. Students seem largely unable to assess how well or poorly they have comprehended material they have just read. **They also tend to be overconfident in newly learned skills, at times because the common educational practice of massed training appears to promote rapid acquisition of skills—as well as self-confidence—but not necessarily the retention of skill.***"

Finally, this journal tackles the implications for the workplace:

> *"Flawed self-assessments arise all the way up the corporate ladder. Employees tend to overestimate their skill, making it difficult to give meaningful feedback. CEOs also display overconfidence in their judgments, particularly when stepping into new markets or novel projects."*

The researchers summed up their conclusions by using a witty quote from one of our founding fathers, Benjamin Franklin:

> ***"There are three things extremely hard: steel, a diamond, and to know one's self."***

Pathetically Apathetic

I guess this means we're not as good as we think we are. I don't know, I have to believe most people are good, right?

Let's break this down further with some hypotheticals. Let's say you're walking down the streets of a big city, Detroit, for example. You've just spent a couple hours at the Art Institute of Detroit, enthralled by the massive canvases and archeological preservations. Many of these items are several hundred years old and you now feel more intelligent and superior after visiting an art museum.

After the art history museum, you take a Lyft downtown for a great meal. While you walk along the street enroute to the restaurant, a little kid is trying to present you a toy. The kid wants you to pay $10 for a trinket that funds some organization. The kid is also super cute.

A Room in the Art Institute of Detroit

An Introduction to Apathy

Do you give the kid $10 for the trinket? What if it was a beggar? A scruffy, old guy who hasn't showered in a month and there's a stench reeking from their presence. He's got a sign that says he's a veteran who needs money. Do you give him money?

Here's another scenario: You scroll through Facebook on a normal weekday. As you swipe through the various posts, you notice that your friend has suffered a recent injury. In order to raise the necessary money to pay off a surgery, he creates a GoFundMe page. You see the Facebook post, you see his injury (it's not pretty) and you remember him being a decent dude. Do you give him some money?

In any of these hypotheticals, you could've said, "Yes." Personally, I've given money to a beggar or two on the street. I've given money to a kid in Detroit. I might do it again. That validates me as a good person, right?

But really, we can recognize so-called "good people" in our lives, right? These are the folks that volunteer for unpaid projects and charities. They post online about doing benefit relief trips. They are probably firefighters or policemen or veterans or something else seemingly noble. They share experiences that end up in crazy positive stories. You know that they genuinely care about kids in wheelchairs, because you see them playing with kids in wheelchairs. They teach mentally disabled kids as a profession. If you don't know someone like this personally, you can watch people like "Mr. Beast" on Youtube giving away $20,000 to a waitress for a glass of water.

Now THAT'S a good person, right? They obviously have some natural instinct that makes them "care more" than we do. Am I serving in some local organization to feed poor people in an assembly line?

Do I consistently participate in acts of charity for random people? Nope, I do not.

So this begs me to ask myself an offensive question. Am I really a good person?

Yeah, come on! Of course I'm a good person! Doesn't this bar seem a little too high? Should we really expect everyone to start going on charity food drives and have a can-do attitude all the time? We can't magically turn into Buddy the Elf here. We've got other things to worry about. We have bills to pay, student loan debt that's always there, annoying family members we'd rather not be related to, and jobs to not get fired from! Aren't we doing a pretty good job as it is?

How does a guy like Justin Wren, the MMA and Wrestling World Champion, create an organization that drills water wells in a forgotten community out in the Democratic Republic of Congo? There are other guys like David Green, the CEO of Hobby Lobby, who caps his salary and spends the rest of it to build orphanages all over the world. On top of that, my own cousin flew out to Uganda to work as a speech pathologist for people who can't afford the service! Who even does that??

In this book, I want to paint an extremely clear picture about a harsh truth. **Most people are apathetic about their own lives, and the world's problems.** A lot of people just don't care and live mediocre lives. Others will seemingly care, but it's only to talk a big game. They'll discuss these big issues and their own ideas on how to solve them on group chats, dinners, social media and social gatherings. Others will even take action, which is great! The problem is the action they take is infrequent and really doesn't do a whole lot to positively improve the situation.

An Introduction to Apathy

There's a cognitive dissonance we need to deal with here. A majority of us believe we are great people who care about each other. Look, nobody likes the fact that women are being taken into the sex trade or that infants are being abandoned in trash dumps. We see the negative headlines and we collectively sigh. We might even do a little reading and talk amongst ourselves about how bad things are. We join rallies when it's popular. We say things like, "If I were in the Oval Office, here's what I would do…"

But deep down, in that dark reality nobody wants to acknowledge, **our actions haven't reflected the thoughts, words or social media posts we blast.** No matter what the conversation is, there's a little more that's required out of us, on an individual and communal level, in order to see the change we complain about.

So let me ask this offensive question again. Am I a good person? Are we good people?

Here's my personal definition of who I believe good people are. **I believe you're a good person if you live an intentional life. If you live a life that's dedicated to improving yourself, the world around you or you've built a life you're satisfied with.** Please understand, what the world doesn't need are more disgruntled, irritated and dysfunctional people who can't seem to find contentment with their lives, no matter what they do.

As our great friend Ben Franklin stressed earlier, there's a dramatic difference between someone who knows themselves and someone who does not. If you know that you can't become a great advocate to solve peace in the Middle East because you need to pay off that car debt, then that's great. Pay off that car debt! If you know that you just don't care about abortion rights, even though your liberal compadres want you to care, then put your care into something else. Come to terms with the reality of your life and be happy with it! And if you're not happy, what will you do to solve your lack of joy in life?

A key question that you should ponder throughout the book is, **"When is it important to care about others and when is it important to care about yourself?"** We really do have our own problems to deal with. I'd argue (and will continue to argue), that it's often better to see yourself personally develop and pursue the accomplishment of your own life goals before tackling the world's problems. **By solving your own problems and becoming a more awesome human being, you're actually helping the world.** You're not being part of the problem.

Before we get too far, I want to encourage you to not lose hope in humanity. There are great people in the world, but you will continue to read negative statistics and facts about the realities of humanity. Once we're done together, my hope is that you'll truly be able to identify the clear differences between someone who intentionally cares and someone who's, really, still quite apathetic. There's a real difference between a driven person and a drifting person. **There are very clear distinctions between apathetic people and non-apathetic people.**

The world has a lot of problems. Your country has problems, your state has problems, your city has problems and the local beggar on your street corner has problems. You have problems, and so do I. What is tangibly being done to solve these problems? **Furthermore, should we really care? Do we even want to care?**

If you're someone like me, who just wants to figure out how to practically care more, this is a great book for you. Whether it's about the global water crisis or simply increasing the size of your paycheck, it's time we cared a little more. Not by sharing a little Facebook post about what we want to see happen, but by actually doing the steps it takes to make it really happen. It's about time you got the education they won't teach you in schools to practically give a crap. Because, without this education, we'll keep living our pathetically apathetic lives as usual...and that won't solve anything.

CHAPTER 1

Solving Problems 101 - It's Simple, But Difficult for Most

So, you've got a problem. Someone you know is dealing with a problem and you want to help them out. You could've just picked up the book because it's an interesting title. Whatever the case is, you're likely here to know how to address and solve whatever is bothering you in your life. I'll break down exactly what you need to do, right now.

First Step: Specifically identify all the things you want to solve. Write down everything that's bothering you on a whiteboard or a piece of paper or on a document. I prefer a whiteboard because it's big and tangible. This could be about your own physical health, your financial stability, the health of other people or a more large-scale problem.

Second Step: Find out how to solve the problems you just wrote down. What do you need to do first to solve the problem? What do you need to start doing to improve things like your faith, family, finances, friends, fitness or fun? Read articles online, ask friends, watch Youtube videos and define what the first steps are to take action.

Third Step: Schedule when and how frequently you will take action. Break out a calendar and to-do list and schedule specifically when you will take action on these issues. For example, put in your calendar from 8 am to 10 am to do nothing else except finish that crossword puzzle. Without scheduling time to solve your problems, you'll constantly try to "find the time." **Trust me, you'll never magically find the time.** Schedule specific blocks of time to focus on your important issues.

Fourth Step: Honor your calendar. Don't put down actions that are unrealistic. If you really won't get up at 6 am to read a book, then don't schedule it in your calendar. **If you actually care about solving the problem, invest the time and the money and the energy to take care of it.** Say "no" to other things going on in your life. Make this issue a major priority by dedicating your scheduled time to it.

Fifth Step: Repeat. Every single morning, create blocks of time to manage your life and the accomplishment of your goals. Create a new to-do list every morning to track all the to-do items you need to get to-done. When plans do not go the way you wanted them to, don't say "woe is me" and stop. Create a new plan the next morning to make sure the problem you faced yesterday doesn't happen again. Through this consistency, you will chip away at the problems. If you never stop, you will, sooner or later, overcome whatever obstacle is in front of you.

That's it.

Yep. There's nothing else. These are the simple steps to address any kind of issue you are bothered by. Now go out there and make it happen!

...but wait...is that really it? Just use a calendar, make to-do lists and spend time every morning to figure out your plan for the day? There has got to be more. How can I figure out how to start my own business and ensure that it's actually successful? Can't you tell me the 14-step process to adequately discipline my kids? Isn't there some "secret" solution that will solve my problems quickly? And what if the plan doesn't go well in the beginning? What if it takes too long to solve my problems? What if it's just too hard and I lose motivation?

Pathetically Apathetic

• • • •

At the core of every problem, it really is as simple as the previous five steps. You can read books about how to grow a business, watch videos with interviews on how other entrepreneurs did it, listen to helpful podcasts and attend seminars with other business owners. No matter how complicated and intricate we want the plan to be, it boils down to these five steps:

- Identify
- Plan
- Schedule
- Execute
- Repeat

In the *Lean Startup*, Eric Reis discusses that the process is to (1) Build, (2) Measure and (3) Learn. You'll also find acronyms like PDCA, standing for (1) Plan, (2) Do, (3) Check and (4) Act, which apparently originated from Toyota's lean manufacturing production system. There's plenty of other books and teachings that essentially express the same message. **Determine what you want, figure out how to get there, act on the plan and refine it to consistently get better results.**

In the last few chapters of this book, starting with chapter 9, we go a little deeper and illustrate practical examples of what it looks like to live a good, non-apathetic lifestyle. You can jump ahead if you really want to, in case you want an abridged version of this book.

For the first eight chapters, I want to dive into something that's more important than implementing the actual steps. Because, honestly, you could find the specific steps to a more meaningful and impactful life in lots of places. There have been books for more than a hundred years on how to do a better job at living.

And that, right there, is why I'm writing this book.

To be fully transparent, I'm writing this book because I think it'd be great to become a ghostwriter. I enjoy the thought of helping people put their writing ideas onto paper and helping them communicate their wisdom and insights in a captivating manner. It's a challenging task I actually enjoy. Writing is not a laborious activity for me, and many people find writing an extraordinarily painful experience. Writing books for people is a goal I have in mind for my life, so I need to obviously write my first book!

But, see, why am I able to write this book in one year, with a full-time job and other obligations, while so many others fail to even get a first draft done of their book? It's not like I'm some special guy here. I don't have a motivational story to tell you and I wasn't born with a magical amount of willpower. I wasn't pressured to write a book like this. More often than not, people ask about what "qualifies" me to write a book about apathy at the age of 25. But, as I mentioned in the Introduction, I did one thing that's very significant. **I changed from being an apathetic person to a caring, non-apathetic person.**

This is the key topic of this entire book. **Most people are collectively, pathetically apathetic about their lives and about the world's problems.** Even if we wanted to do something about it, our situation doesn't actually change and we keep living our same old, unsatisfactory lives. That's the reason why I say "pathetically" apathetic. **Any attempt we make to improve ourselves looks pathetic.** This is profound and the issue deserves to be thoroughly dissected.

Pathetically Apathetic

How We're Collectively Apathetic

It's become so habitual for people to start new things, get caught up in the flashy new idea, promote a big launch for some "thought-provoking" initiative, and then a week, a month, a few months or a couple years later, get really bored with it and stop. It could be with a new smartphone or a new car or a new podcast or a new book or a new college course or a new apartment or a new job or a new roommate or even a new spouse! I mean, come on, the records show from the National Survey of Family Growth that almost 50% of all marriages in the United States still end in divorce. Everybody loves the new thing and hates the old normal thing they've been doing. Even if that old thing still did a great job, they want to switch to the newest thing.

It's so common for people to get apathetic about their current circumstances. They either keep changing things or just settle for something lackluster. Why should we switch to a new job or a new house or throw away the perfectly good phone? Is it really because we're just bored? Is it really because it's not working anymore? **Or do most people really have a deep, psychological problem that keeps them from ever living a truly fulfilling, happy life?**

What's my goal here? I said it in the Introduction and I'll likely say it 137 more times. **I would love for you and anyone who reads this book to understand that too many people suffer from cognitive dissonance.** Are you tracking with me? You know that situation where someone says they will do something, but they don't? When someone believes something in one instant and then goes the opposite direction in another situation? When you get pumped up about a cool activity today, but you then think it's the worst activity ever the next day? These are all situations that cause cognitive dissonance.

After so many instances of cognitive dissonance, we become apathetic. Apathy is, simply put, a lack of interest or concern. This isn't necessarily a negative attribute, but it becomes negative when people are always apathetic. Once it becomes a consistent character trait, it becomes terribly difficult to make any changes in your life. Instead of having a "lack of interest" in golf or accounting, you have a lack of interest in everything, and that leaves you pathetically failing to try and accomplish anything.

With one bad apple, this doesn't destroy the world. There's always going to be one lazy bum in your neighborhood. When more and more people share the same stories of cognitive dissonance and apathy through we collectively become apathetic. This is why you can find so many solvable issues, that, if enough people just cared to live better or act more appropriately, wouldn't be issues anymore.

Because we're all apathetic, we are all very understanding of each other's apathy. If you're late for a party and you blame the traffic, "we understand." If you didn't get something done that you planned to get done because today you were super busy, "we can relate." If you forgot to call back your friend about some trip you wanted to plan, "no worries, I'm sure you were thinking about other, more important things." Nobody's perfect right? So let's not get so serious and just do the best that we can. Do we really want people to start getting anal about everything and expect perfection out of everyone?

Our culture is very understanding of people's shortcomings. We live with it. Why? Well, because we don't want to be that dude that's always pointing out someone being three minutes late. We don't want to be the hardass who calls out someone for not bringing the food they said they were going to bring to the party. "It's all cool man!" We can live through it and still be happy, right?

The problem is, all of these small, seemingly innocent situations, in a very subtle way, encourage cognitive dissonance and collective apathy.

• • • •

But, I must ask, who am I to make these claims about our society? What gives me the right to declare that everyone is collectively, pathetically apathetic? I'm a 25 year-old white guy who had it pretty easy growing up. Sure, I decided three years ago to finally get serious with my life, but that's not really a motivational story. Did I surmount great obstacles of poverty and a life of tragedy to finally bring you this amazing book? Not at all.

Neither did Bill Gates. As Malcolm Gladwell discusses in his book, *Outliers*, Bill Gates had a lot of things go right in his life. He grew up in wealth. He started early in his fascination with engineering and naturally kept it up. He was given access to some of the best computers as early as 1968, when he was just eight years old. Most colleges didn't own computers in the 1960s. A ton of stuff went well for this guy to give him a running start. Some might even say that it's hard to look at Bill Gates as an encouraging, motivating story.

You wouldn't call Bill Gates an apathetic guy, though. He's a man who founded one of the largest charitable organizations ever. He's a man who spent decades of deeply focused, passionate time developing a world-class knowledge of computer circuitry. He didn't harbor it for himself, but shared it so everyone could massively improve their lives. He's a man who cares immensely about keeping his dominance in the business world. He is not an apathetic man.

Neither is Blake Mycoskie, the founder of TOMS Shoes. This company is a hallmark example of an organization that does business for a cause. You buy a shoe and you give a shoe to someone in need. It's such a simple way to justify your shopping spree while satisfying someone's feet in Africa with shoes. Blake Mycoskie was raised by an orthopedic surgeon, though, and went to Southern Methodist University on a tennis scholarship. SMU is not a cheap college and his parents paid for him to go to college! During his time there, he also founded a $1 million laundry company and always had a knack for being entrepreneurial. Is his story a "started from the bottom, now we're here" kind of narrative? Doesn't seem like it; but, what's immensely obvious is this man was not apathetic about his life. He got after it and continues to get after it!

Martin Luther King Jr. was on a quest to liberate blacks in America from the stronghold of poverty, and was willing to die doing it. So was Nelson Mandella, who helped alleviate a racial conflict in South Africa of his own. There are also Mahatma Gandhi, Mother Teresa, and countless others you might think of who fought for noble causes. They obviously illustrate immense compassion for those in need. So much so, they all died doing it.

The Reality of Solving a Big Problem

A lot of people fantasize about solving large problems like this. Are you willing to become the next crusader for a social cause? Will you create the next business that transforms the economy? You certainly could. You could be like many of the bright-eyed college students out there who say they will "solve world hunger" or "fight for the forgotten." Justin Wren certainly did.

Pathetically Apathetic

It took Justin Wren several years and several life-threatening circumstances to become the "Big Pygmy." It's the typical rollercoaster story of great highs and lows you could make a movie out of. Ever since 2013, he has dedicated the rest of his life to bringing the Pygmy tribe in Africa out of poverty and slavery. He drills wells for clean water, organizes the purchasing of land so they have rights to property, and seeks funding to support all of these beneficial activities to save the livelihoods of these "forgotten" people. Because of this, you could consider Justin Wren to be the exact opposite of someone who lives a life of apathy.

What you should know is that Justin Wren was once a very apathetic man. For years, due to drug overdoses, wild partying, and deep-seated depression from years of bullying, he threw away his religion and lost his care for the world. He lost interest in his friends and family, and disconnected. You would never have imagined that he would become one of the modern day, altruistic heroes of this generation. There's a time in Justin Wren's life that's particularly dark in Chapter 9 of his book, *Fight for the Forgotten*, where he's kicked off of his fighting team and tailspins into months of aimlessness.

The coach of his crew was the only guy that stood by him, but everyone else wanted Justin off the team. In a one-on-one meeting with Justin, here's what the coach had to say: "*Justin, you've put me in a really tough position (he started somberly). We've taken a vote and everyone has voted you off the team, everyone but me. However, I can't go against the other guys.* **We just can't have your name attached to ours**."

Ouch! They can't be associated with Justin Wren's name anymore? Sheesh... what did Wren do to deserve this? Wren explains: "*They all knew I came in to train hungover, alcohol sweating from my pores, but they didn't know I was sometimes buzzed and high--not the safest conditions when you're punching and choking out teammates."*

Justin was a successful fighter, though! At the time, he had a record of 10-2. He was a big name in this growing sport. This was all while having these drug issues. His problems were too deep and apparent to ignore, and that caused his team to kick him off, which sent him into a downward spiral of depression. This excerpt below from his book, shows just how deeply he was into his drug abuse:

"The more depressed I got, the more I used. I rotated cocaine back into the mix and the wear started to show. On the morning of my next fight for the Ring of Fire, a prestigious Denver promotion, I was in the emergency room throwing up. I'd have some issues with my back and had gone heavy on the pills of late. The doctor thought I had a stomach virus, but I had no doubt it was from the drugs. The doctor gave me three bags of IV fluid and urged me not to fight that night, but that didn't stop me. During the fight, a wave of anger overtook me and I violently slammed my opponent to the mat. I was this irate person. After I won, I raced back to my hotel room to celebrate with my drugs. I didn't know it at the time, but this would be my last fight with Grudge [his fighting team] *in my corner.*

The next two months of my life remain a blur. I get cloudy flashes here and there, but nothing concrete. I started skipping Grudge sessions and really plugged into the drug community in the mountains where I lived. I hitchhiked and caught rides from drug house to drug house, drinking, smoking, and taking hallucinogens like mushrooms and Ecstasy. I don't think I've ever done meth, but I really couldn't tell you, to be honest. It's possible I tried it while in this blurry fog. I woke up in some strange houses, usually one of the worst of the bunch. The other druggies would end up having to take care of me. On one night, I remember I made a concerted effort to end my life with a mix of pills, pot, mushrooms, and a half bottle of 190-proof Everclear.

Pathetically Apathetic

I remember my disappointment when I woke up the next day, still alive."

Somehow, even in his darkest hour, he miraculously picked himself up. He would turn back to Christianity, after abandoning it due to terrible experiences in the church of his youth. He would find a calling for these lost people in the deep, untouched Congo and fulfill his true purpose. He would truly realize the gravity of his mistakes and do a complete 180 to become the "Big Pygmy."

Justin Wren, towering over Pygmy tribe hunters

The dramatic stories about people transforming their lives for good sound awesome. It fills stadiums with enthusiastic cheers. It gets millions of views on Youtube and Facebook. Everyone loves a good transformation story, because they really are so inspiring. There are many examples of people who, as Dr. Jordan Peterson calls it, "slayed the dragon in the gold mine" or "saved their father from the belly of a whale."

These great people go onstage to share their story. They write books to communicate the deep details of their message. They create podcasts to continually give you the newest "pick-me-up", encouraging episodes about fixing your life. The overall message from all these people? "If I can do this, then you can too!"

But, I don't know. It doesn't seem like enough people are really buying into it.

The Good Stories Don't Seem To Matter

I mean, people buy these stories all the time with their money. Those stadiums are packed with people who need to "seize their destiny." Those books are sold all day long because it gives people "the secrets to success." Why do you think shows like Oprah, Dr. Oz and Ellen kept getting great ratings? Everybody likes a nice, heartwarming story. Why are some of the most viral videos about people who do remarkably good things? Why do the heroes always win in the end? Why does the guy always get the girl or vice versa? Why are Hallmark movies still successful? Because of all these great, heartwarming and encouraging resources we can find, shouldn't more people be making positive momentum with their lives?

Unfortunately, we don't change. If this is the last page you read before getting bored and losing interest, please realize that you could gain all of the world's knowledge, wisdom and insights. You could attend every self-help seminar money can buy. You could read all of the books about all of the secrets to success. You could listen to hundreds of thousands of interviews with multi-million dollar, successful people. You could be given every advantage and every opportunity in the world to live a phenomenal life. AND YET, a man can still wake up at 50 years old and wonder where the hell his life went. AND YET, a woman can be divorced three times and bank on this fourth marriage to "be the one that lasts." AND YET, a man can go from dead-end job to dead-end job and blame the world for all of his life problems. AND YET, a woman can understand that she has dire problems with her physical health and family, but not take action to solve them.

It's a much deeper and socially-accepted problem that exists here. **It's a massive cultural acceptance of a lackluster average that I believe few recognize.** Even if we recognize it, we are unwilling to fix the issues because it's too troublesome or will stir up some tough conversations. It's the constant lack of honor toward our word. It's the lack of trust in others. It's a lack of commitment for the long haul. It's the habitual drifting that keeps people from getting really good at something. **It's an apathy toward life that everyone seems to accept, a collective apathy, if you will.**

I've got news for you. There isn't some "secret concept" that I'm waiting to reveal about the "mysteries of success." I told you right at the beginning what the simple steps are! **These principles have been known for centuries!** They aren't outdated, and they don't need a new mobile app so it works for "our generation."

If you really want to change your life and make great improvements, I encourage you to start with two books and actually finish them. Dale Carnegie's, *How to Win Friends and Influence People,* and Napoleon Hill's, *Think and Grow Rich,* are two of the most pivotal, earliest books written to improving your life (other than the Bible and other religious or philosophical texts). With both books having been written in the 1930s, they are some of the first popular pieces of literature dedicated to life success.

Solving Problems 101

I promise you that if you just read these books and actually applied them to your life, that's all the help you would need.

Hold on... am I actually encouraging you not to read my book?

If you drop this book in a nearby river, pick up these two books I just suggested, and actually apply these books to your life, then I will be satisfied. You will become a more awesome person and you will thank me as a result. My goal isn't for you to become a fan of me and prop me up as some "self-help genius." Because I'm not! Remember, I'm just a 25 year-old guy who wants to write books for a living.

My entire goal is to have you realize that we all have some form of cognitive dissonance with our lives. We all find some parts of our lives unsatisfactory. We keep saying that these issues are issues, but where is the action? Where is the change? Where is the implementation of these "secrets to success?" Why are there only a few people who truly turn their lives around for the long haul, while everyone else looks on in disbelief? When so many people are starting things and stopping things out of boredom, why are there only a few that genuinely put in the action to transform their lives? Why do people still buy this stuff over and over and over again if nothing continues to happen? What is the problem?

Most people don't actually care.

CHAPTER 2:

*Most Don't Care
(The Undeniable Reality)*

This book isn't starting with a lot of encouragement. This likely isn't a book that causes you to feel all warm and fuzzy inside. But, you know what, we could start being intentional right now about, not only our problems, but the world's problems. What does that actually look like?

Let's take a moment to highlight just three different problems listed as some key issues the world faces. Bright-eyed college students and disgruntled 40 year-olds talk about how they want to make an impact with their lives. Many of you who read this book want to do the same! Well...what can actually be done to solve some issues? You already know people talk a big game about how crucial it is to stop world hunger, climate change and countless other problems. What steps can you actually take?

THREE PROBLEMS YOU COULD START SOLVING TODAY

1. Climate Change

<u>What is the Issue?</u>

Climate Change can be defined as scientifically researched observations about our planet, which determine that the Earth's climate is changing more rapidly than at any previous point in modern human history. While changes in climate are widely regarded as normal occurrences, Climate Change indicates violent fluctuations in our ecosystem that are caused by human actions. The main issues involve the overall increased temperature of the Earth, the pollution of oxygen in our atmosphere and the increased frequency of natural disasters. Many skeptics question the validity that any human activities actually cause more frequent natural disasters, but advocates for slowing Climate Change say that human activities, such as the emission of heat-trapping greenhouse gases from fossil fuel combustion, deforestation and land-use change, are the primary drivers of Climate Change observed in the industrial era.

Why is This Bad?

Since this issue spans the entire globe, studies have found that it affects various aspects of our livelihood. Our overall human health and wellbeing take a toll due to extreme elemental disasters, such as raging wildfires. Rapid changes in the ecosystem also gravely affect the security of the world's food supply straining water quality and supply due to frequent sediment and contaminant concentrations. Our water is getting worse and worse, with decreasing amounts left for us. The world's massive amount of consumption and overproduction also take a heavy toll on the climate. According to scientific findings, activities like overfishing, fossil fuel pollution of the air and deforestation cause wear and tear to our environment.

This is a massively researched, dense topic, and would take an entire book to unpack. So, to make a crystal clear point on the scientific reality of Climate Change, the IPCC (the Intergovernmental Panel on Climate Change) produced its Fifth Assessment Report on the climate.

This research consisted of a group of 1,300 independent scientific experts, from countries all over the world, under the auspices of the United Nations. Their combined research showed, *"there's a more than 95 percent probability that human activities over the past 50 years have warmed our planet."*

<u>What Can You Do?</u>

Due to the magnitude of a problem like "Climate Change," we can't simply take one big swing at the issue. It would be illogical to band together with your friends and say, "Hey guys, let's STOP CLIMATE CHANGE TODAY!" We need to be smart and start somewhere realistic with our actions.

• • • •

I must take a pause and emphasize an important point in regard to solving any problem. With every issue you're trying to solve, personal or global, **you have to start somewhere.** You begin with what you can handle, get really good at that thing consistently, then move on to the next thing. **Start somewhere, then build off of that success.** Here are a couple short, sweet quotes from partners in my consulting firm that stress this point:

"Be fruitful; then multiply."

Tim Redmond
(My boss, who built up an accounting software company from scratch to $40 million/year, then sold it to Intuit in 2001)

Most Don't Care

"Nail it first, then scale it."

Dr. Robert Zoeller

(Owner of several multi-million dollar businesses and his optometrist offices - Dr. Zoellner & Associates grosses the highest retail sales/square foot of any optometrist in the United States)

Tim Redmond's point is to be fruitful with whatever you start with. I've got a whole chapter later about this point (chapter 10), but in his own book, *Power to Create*, he emphasizes that you likely already have the tools available to start. When you start, make sure it's actually fruitful before growing and expanding your efforts. Here's a section from Tim's book where he uses scripture from the Bible to solidify his quote:

> *"In the age of instant, we think success suddenly happens to the lucky few who find their way to abundance. That is not the pattern of success in the Bible and rarely how it goes today. In a passage known by few and quoted by fewer still, God dictated the start-small strategy for the Israelites coming into the Promised Land. He told them, 'Little by little I will drive them out from before you, until you have increased, and inherit the land. [Exodus 23:30]' He warned them that if they expanded too quickly, their land would 'grow up in weeds and the wild animals would take over. [Exodus 23:29]'* **God knew what they couldn't manage well, they would lose."**

For Climate Change and the next couple issues, I will list out action steps that seem small and insignificant. You've been preached to go for the big solutions and completely solve the issue in one big sweeping motion. **In reality, you can't solve Climate Change, drug abuse**

in America, gambling problems or any other dilemma without starting small and being fruitful with those first steps. With consistent effort, patience, and fruitfulness, as Tim described, we can manage more responsibility to invoke change.

Anyway, let's continue.

• • • •

The David Suzuki Foundation, an organization founded to provide additional research, evidence and education on the subject of preserving our environment, gives ten ways to begin to get active in helping slow Climate Change. In David Suzuki's words,

> *"In a world of more than seven billion people, each of us is a drop in the bucket. But with enough drops, we can fill any bucket."*
>
> DAVID SUZUKI
> (P.H.D. in Zoology and host of the popular and long-running CBC Television science program *The Nature of Things*, seen in over 40 countries. He's been the host for over 40 years, since 1979.)

The first recommended step? Demand that change happens with your elected representatives. This will become a recurring first step for many of these issues, but by constantly badgering your senators, congressmen and women, and even your city councils, you can be the change agent for any cause. So, start the calling campaign and email campaign and knock on their doors for some action!

But, before you even talk with elected representatives, you should probably come prepared with things to tangibly do. Even if you do

Most Don't Care

come to your government with proposals, they will be slow to act on anything. So, here are some simple suggestions that lower your energy consumption, a major factor in the pollution of our environment (provided by the David Suzuki Foundation):

- » Change to energy-efficient light bulbs.
- » Install a heat pump in your home.
- » Unplug computers, TVs and other electronics when you're not using them.
- » Wash clothes in cold or warm water (not hot).
- » Hang-dry your clothes when you can and use dryer balls when you can't.
- » Install a programmable thermostat.
- » Look for the Energy Star label when buying new appliances.
- » Winterize your home to prevent heat from escaping and try to keep it cool in the summer without an air conditioner.
- » Take public transit.
- » Ride a bike or advocate for bike lanes in your community.
- » Car-share.
- » Switch to an electric or hybrid vehicle.
- » Fly less (if you do fly, make sure you offset your emissions).
- » Eat more meat-free meals.
- » Buy organic and local whenever possible.
- » Don't waste food.

With some simple Googling, I was able to find all of this information in less than 30 minutes. The information is so readily available. Do you remember when people needed to go to a library to find relevant information? Do you even remember that people needed to go to libraries? Who even goes to libraries??

If a topic like Climate Change speaks to you, stop reading and start Googling. Go on the rabbit trail and grow an obsession about whatever curious thoughts you have. As we'll discuss later in the book (chapter 5), this is a huge factor in eliminating apathy from our lives.

2. World Hunger

<u>What is the Issue?</u>

The World Bank tells us that, *"since 1990, the world has reduced the number of people who live in extreme poverty by over half.* ***But that still leaves 767 million people living on the edge of survival with less than $1.90 a day.***" Africa and Asia deal with the worst hunger problems. Almost 23% of Africa's Sub-Saharan population suffers from undernourishment and almost 2/3rds of all malnourished people in the world live in Asia.

<u>Why is This Bad?</u>

You obviously know why this is bad, but the Freedom From Hunger organization explains that, *"when a child is undernourished her immune system is weakened and she can't fight off common, preventable illnesses like diarrhea or pneumonia."* To give the best singular statistic about the status of world hunger, Freedom From Hunger also states:

> ***"Globally, one in nine people in the world today (795 million) are undernourished."***

For people in poverty, in many cases, their mainstream of income and nutrition is through farming. However, for numerous reasons, they can't sell the produce, receive the credit to fund their operations or compete against larger producers. Since many of these impoverished people live in rural areas, they literally can't get to the markets to sell produce. In addition to farming challenges, these hungry people also aren't fully educated on best practice health moves like handwashing or how to have safe drinking water. Many don't have safe drinking water! Because of this, people are easily at risk of common diseases and illnesses that fully nourished people can fight off.

<u>What Can You Do?</u>

Partner with an organization. There are so many non-profits, NGOs and organizations that fight to end world hunger. Remember, the statistics show we've reduced the number of people who live in extreme poverty by more than half. GO HUMANITY! But, why stop there?

Through your active participation in events, consistent funding for support and promoting victories in ending world hunger on social media, you can become a vocal agent for this cause! The more and more you contribute with time, funds and voicing your concerns, the more you will become a more powerful agent for this positive change.

Here are ten organizations you can get plugged into RIGHT NOW:

- » Mercy Corps - https://www.mercycorps.org/
- » US AID - https://www.usaid.gov/
- » Feed the Future - https://www.feedthefuture.gov/
- » Rise Against Hunger - https://www.riseagainsthunger.org/
- » Freedom from Hunger - https://www.freedomfromhunger.org/
- » Bread for the World - https://www.bread.org/
- » The Hunger Project - https://www.thp.org/
- » Action Against Hunger - https://www.actionagainsthunger.org/
- » The Salvation Army - https://www.salvationarmy.org/
- » Compassion International - https://www.compassion.com/

You should also research your local food banks and non-profit organizations. Because, while a lot of hunger and undernourishment issues happen in other parts of the globe, you've got hungry people a few blocks from you, too.

Google "local food banks" in your area and see how you can contribute with finances and time!

3. This Book's Lack of Sales

<u>What is the Issue?</u>

I'm a little partial to this "world issue," but my lack of book sales is an issue, nonetheless. The world would be a much better place if I just got more book sales!

<u>Why is This Bad?</u>

Why would it be a better place? The topic of this book is about helping to turn yourself and others from being pathetically apathetic people into compassionate, empathetic people to GET STUFF DONE. Even if it's just to improve how you live, that's success! What would the results be if I sold many copies of this book? And, what if people actually did what was written here?

For kicks and giggles, let's break down the number of "real implementers" of this book, based on the success of New Year's Resolutions. You'll find on *Forbes* and other websites this statistic: "*Only 8% of people keep their New Year's Resolutions.*" So, if the New Year's Resolution was to read this book, **I would theoretically need to sell 100,000 copies of this book if I wanted 8,000 people to become more compassionate and caring with their lives.** That's a lot of books… and only a few books ever sell that many copies.

Most Don't Care

What if I wanted to be a *New York Times* best-selling author? You get onto this list by selling 9,000 copies in the 1st week of the release. Based on 9,000 people buying this book, how many of those 1st week buyers would actually stick to anything in my book? 720 people.

<u>What Can You Do?</u>

Well, you've already become my favorite person in the world by buying this book and getting this far. So, congrats!

Share the book and some notable quotables on your social media! Gift this book to a friend, family member or a random citizen of Earth! What's a better way to say "Merry Christmas" than giving someone a book that tells them how pathetic and uncaring they are as a human being?

Yeah, alright, you might want to be careful with making this a gift, but here's another profound way to promote my book without even promoting it...START BEING COMPASSIONATE. START GIVING A FLIP ABOUT YOUR LIFE. Once people ask you what changed, don't be a butt head. Tell them about this book.

Some Healthy Honesty About Ourselves

I had thoughts and hopes and dreams to do various cool things with my life. I was like every bright-eyed college student who thought they could be the next shining star in this lost world. But, like most of you reading this book, **I had a very tough time finding something to pursue...something to commit to as a passionate desire...as an obsession.** None of my "fun" ideas amounted to any kind of impact, because I never committed to these ideas.

Pathetically Apathetic

I really don't get passionate about things, anyway. I'll have moments where I'm on an emotional high, but those moments are brief. Nothing ever stood out to me and said, "Yeah, that's who I'm gonna be!" I didn't get out of high school wanting to become a lawyer, doctor, plumber or any kind of profession. But, let's be honest, **could you have imagined how you ended up here?**

Where you are now, likely can't be attributed to deep passion or continual ambition. It was likely because you were simply available to do what you're doing now. You weren't deeply empathetic about that drug company's sales, but you needed a job that paid well. You weren't "moved" to become a full-time teacher, but that music degree didn't sign you a music contract, so you took the job. You didn't think of becoming a mechanic, but your dad taught you so much about cars that it was an easy field. **Passion didn't get you to your current spot in life, necessity did.** Besides, Passion is a pretty fickle topic. I would argue that the "super compassionate" people can't use just pure passion. Emotional highs are unreliable and wavering.

The caring, passionate people you see today have tapped into a type of commitment that transcends most of us. They've tapped into a self-motivation that surpasses normalcy. They realized what a great goal looks like and they seized it, no questions asked. One of the most impactful quotes I've ever heard about motivation and commitment came from Andrew Carnegie.

> *"People who are unable to motivate themselves must be content with mediocrity."*
>
> ANDREW CARNEGIE
> (Who became one of the richest men in American history due to his contributions in expanding the American steel industry)

Most Don't Care

Me having a tough conversation with myself

I'm sorry. That's so good, we need to read it again. *"People who are unable to motivate themselves **must be content with mediocrity.**"*

Being content with mediocrity? Ouch! That's so harsh! As I broke down what this meant, I came to realize that **I was secretly content with mediocrity.** Does it matter if I lived a more comfortable and secure life financially than most? Does it matter if I stayed thin and had friends and worked at a job that provided opportunities to advance and grow? Does it matter that I had very few traumatic moments in my past? **None of these variables matter because, in my 22 year-old mind, I still considered myself mediocre.**

Pathetically Apathetic

While I could settle for earning a pretty good wage as a recent college graduate, **I was doing nothing to work towards a wage that I wanted to earn in the future, in a career I really wanted to work in.** I considered myself mediocre, because I was doing nothing to proactively get to my goals. There were no actions behind my words. Even if I did put forth action, I didn't even know what my goals were! This quote was quite a shock to my system. To realize that I'm actually content with mediocrity?

If you had a passion and a goal in mind, you could easily spend 30 minutes Googling the topic and come up with what you need to do. You could call someone who knows what to do, or at least point you in the right direction. Remember, the steps are simple! You identify the desire, plan steps, schedule the implementation, execute the plan, and repeat. **But just like me, most people are living content with mediocrity and we don't have the backbone to address this reality head-on**. It doesn't matter what cause or mission it's for, facing reality is tough for folks to swallow.

Since you're reading this book, it's obvious something isn't going the way you want it to. You don't have the contentment and purpose in your life that others "seem" to have. Those three world problems I broke down sound great to get passionate about, but you haven't made any headway with any passion. You have issues in your life that you can't get your butt behind. The title, *Pathetically Apathetic*, caught your attention because deep down, it may describe you...it described me for 22 years of my life!

This is why **I sympathize with your lack of purpose and contentment.** I'll remind you that you're not the only person dealing with this cognitive dissonance. Most people are at the exact same spot you're at.

Most Don't Care

You're in a large sea of fish being constantly pushed by emotional tides.

I really need to hammer this home, because that's what it takes to convince even the most cynical people that a problem exists. So, if I need to share 25 statistics and studies in one giant list to prove my point, that people need to stop being pathetically apathetic, then so be it!

25 Reasons Why We're Pathetically Apathetic

1. **75% of employees steal from the workplace.** According to a 2015 study from the US Chamber of Commerce, *"75% of employees steal from the workplace and that most do so repeatedly."*

2. Nearly **95% of all businesses suffer from theft** in the workplace.

3. **A typical organization loses 5% of its annual revenues due to employee fraud.** When CBS News applied this fact to the 2009 Gross World Product *"this figure translates to a potential global fraud loss of more than $2.9 trillion."*

4. **One-third of all U.S. corporate bankruptcies are directly caused by employee theft.**

5. On top of all this, an INC. Magazine article puts this in a big perspective. *"The U.S. Chamber of Commerce estimates that **theft by employees costs American companies $20 billion to $40 billion a year.** To pay for it, every man and woman working in America today contributes more than $400 per year."*

6. **Smartphones Are Making Us Dumb.** In a Psychology Today article from 2015, an experiment about productivity in the workplace with smartphones was described. They had

some participants work while their phones were stowed out of sight and some participants with their phones in the line of sight. *"Compared to those whose phones were stowed out of view, **participants whose phones sat on their desk performed nearly 20% worse.**"*

7. **Most Employees Only Work for 3 Hours Per Day.** The Bureau of Labor Statistics shared that workers only work for approximately two hours and 53 minutes.

8. **We Don't Care About Geography.** The Harvard School of Education found that over 50% of the 18-24 year-old Americans surveyed by National Geographic couldn't find the state of New York on a map.

9. **Employees Actually Watch Adult Content While at Work.** Newsweek revealed that a quarter of employees who use the internet during work watch porn. Apparently, pornsites are actually the most active during office hours, more than any other time of the day.

10. **A Quarter of All Women Suffered Child Abuse.** A study put together by the Centers for Disease Control and Prevention showed that 1 in 4 women and 1 in 13 men were sexually abused before the age of 18.

11. **There Are a Lot of Crazy People Out There.** According to reports published by the ADA National Network in 2018, researchers found that, in a nationally representative study of Americans ages 15 to 54, 18% of those who were employed said they experienced symptoms of a mental health disorder in the previous month.

12. **There Aren't Many Fatherly Role Models.** According to research conducted by the U.S. Census Bureau, nearly 24 million children in America (1 out of 3) live in homes where the biological father is absent.

13. Furthermore, children with fatherless homes are 2x more likely to drop out of high school, 2x more likely to suffer from obesity and 7x more likely to be involved in a teen pregnancy.

14. **We're Not Getting Smarter.** In an article posted by Michael Winter for USA Today, the College Board now shows that just 40% of the high school seniors met benchmarks for college success on average. **These numbers haven't significantly changed nationwide for more than five years.**

15. **Employees Aren't Engaged in the Workplace.** According to a 2018 Gallup poll, 53% of employees are "not engaged" in the workplace.

16. **We Like it When People Get Hurt.** As early as four years old, research has shown that toddlers experience *Schadenfreude*, the pleasure at another person's distress.

17. In this same research study, children as young as six years old would rather spend money seeing an antisocial puppet being hit than purchasing stickers.

18. **We're Easy to Dehumanize.** As early as five years old, we view out-group faces as less human than in-group faces. **Basically, people who look differently than us are viewed less significantly.**

19. **We're Ready to Blame Others for Our Faults.** Studies done in 2019, identify that *"to save face when things go wrong, people will sometimes shift blame away from themselves by bringing attention to external causes."*

20. **We Don't Like Thinking...Or, At Least, Men Don't.** 67% of male participants and 25% of female participants opted to give themselves unpleasant electric shocks rather than spend 15 minutes in peaceful contemplation.

21. **We are Moral Hypocrites.** In one study, researchers gave people the choice between two tasks, an easy one and a hard one. When they choose a task, the other participant is forced to do the other one. The participants thought it was unfair and selfish when the other participant chose the easy task. But, **when they chose the easy task for themselves, they didn't believe this was morally objectionable.** The study defines this as 'moral hypocrisy,' *"a phenomenon in which individuals judge their own transgressions to be less morally objectionable than the same transgressions enacted by others."*

22. **We Become More Disconnected as We Gain Stature.** A psychologist from Berkeley, Dacher Keltner, conducted research that suggests that **as people rise through the ranks, their ability to maintain personal connection suffers.**

23. The same psychologist also found that **people who have power suffer deficits of empathy**, the ability to read emotions and the ability to adapt behaviors to other people.

24. **We Don't Empathize With Each Other's Pain.** Rachel Ruttan, a researcher and psychologist from the University of Toronto, describes her conclusions about people's empathy for each other.

> She writes, *"We found that **people who have endured challenges in the past** (like divorce or being skipped over for a promotion) **were less likely to show compassion** for someone facing the same struggle, compared with people with no experience in that particular situation."*

25. Rachel and her researchers also found that, *"**people who had overcome a period of unemployment in the past were less compassionate and more judgmental** of the man than people who were currently unemployed or had never been involuntarily unemployed."*

Four Key Reasons For This Reality

Do these 25 reasons really illustrate how our society is collectively, pathetically apathetic? Yes, because if people just took the patience and the time to think about their lives and improve themselves, you wouldn't find such negative realities about our world. People would choose to not get married or have sex, alleviating children from starting on the wrong foot in life. People would actually be wise and save their money so they wouldn't feel obligated to steal from businesses. People would work to advance and prosper, rather than simply "get by." More people would actually be engaged in the workplace, even if it isn't their dream job. **All of these circumstances are a result of us not caring enough, and as a result, living pathetically apathetic lives.**

We keep regressing to a low-standard mean in life. All the self-help books...all the interviews with successful people...all the podcasts about improving our lives...all the conferences we go to...all the religious leaders and teachers...all the motivating quote posters...all the therapy sessions...all the support groups...all the history of great heroes and leaders...it's barely making a dent.

Are we good people? As I defined in the Introduction, **I believe you're a good person if you live a very intentional life, a life that's dedicated to improving yourself and the world around you.** It's not about humanitarian projects. It's not about how many donations you give or how charitable you are. I'm not trying to make you a martyr for a cause. I'm simply illustrating that **there are very clear differences between an apathetic person and a person who cares about what they're doing with their life.**

While you could skip to chapter 9 and read more details about the specific steps to implement, I encourage you to read through these next few chapters. Before you even think about making enhancements to your life, it's pivotal to understand how we got here. Where's the disconnect? Why do people keep falling into this cycle of unmet, hopeful expectations in life? I break this down into four core areas of concern that cause us to be collectively apathetic. **Because, it's more than just a "you" problem—we're all pathetically apathetic.**

- TRUST: THE FIRST DYSFUNCTION
- THE ENORMOUS PROBLEM WITH SAVING THE WORLD
- OBSESSION IS WEIRD
- ENVIRONMENT AND THE MENTORSHIP GAP

Most Don't Care

Pathetically Apathetic

CHAPTER 3:

Trust: The First Dysfunction

The Five Dysfunctions of a Team was a book written by Patrick Lencioni, a business consultant and public speaker. It's been on the best selling lists for The *New York Times, Business Week, Wall Street Journal, and USA Today.* The book has sold over three million copies and continues to be a hallmark piece of literature in the business world and in team building.

The story details a company (DecisionTech) with talented colleagues, but they all work in a company that isn't meeting their hype. They are falling behind competitors who shouldn't be beating them. An outside source, Kathryn, with decades of experience managing teams, comes in to serve as CEO in this challenging time for the company. She was actually called in by the company's current CEO, Jeff, to take the mantle. After her observations during the first month or so, she decides to call an off-site retreat for a weekend with the key team members for the tech company. She's using this retreat to focus on some key issues the team is facing. Kathryn details that there are five dysfunctions with the current team, explaining why their competitors continue to beat them. She uses this retreat and the following years to solve the company's problems.

The first dysfunction Kathryn discusses at the retreat is actually the biggest ingredient for why we're apathetic with our lives. It's one of the

Trust: The First Dysfunction

core reasons for why we continually deal with cognitive dissonance. To help lay the foundation for our chapter, let's turn to an excerpt from *Five Dysfunctions of a Team* on how Kathryn sets the tone for this first dysfunction:

• • • •

Kathryn then turned back to the group. "Over the course of the next two days…you'll notice that none of this is rocket science. **In fact, it will seem remarkably simple on paper. The trick is putting it into practice."**

"Right now **I'd like to start with the first dysfunction: absence of trust."** She turned and wrote the phrase at the bottom of the triangle. The staff members read the words silently, and most of them frowned as if to say, "*Is that all you've got?*"

Kathryn was used to this and continued. "**Trust is the foundation of real teamwork**. And so, the first dysfunction is a failure on the part of team members to understand and open up to one another. And if that sounds touchy-feely, let me explain, because there is nothing soft about it. It is an absolutely critical part of building a team. **In fact, it's probably the most critical.**" Some of the people in the room were clearly in need of an explanation.

"**Great teams do not hold back with one another,**" she said. "**They are unafraid to air their dirty laundry. They admit their mistakes, their weaknesses, and their concerns without fear of reprisal.**" Most of the staff seemed to be accepting the point, but without a lot of enthusiasm.

Kathryn pushed on. "**The fact is, if we don't trust one another—and it seems to me that we don't—then we cannot be the kind of**

team that ultimately achieves results. And so that is where we're going to focus first."

• • • •

We'll go ahead and start here, too.

We Only Want to Trust Ourselves

Our livelihoods are held together by trust. You are currently reading this book because you trust that there is nothing else you must be concerned with. You trust that gravity works so your drink won't float away. You trust that the sun won't burn you to a crisp because you lathered yourself in sunscreen. You trust that the food you just ate at the local food stand in Mexico won't completely destroy your intestines (hopefully). Our trust keeps the world in order.

But here's the problem...

Only 1/3rd of Americans trust each other. In a study done by the General Social Survey, that spans over 40 years, they've found that trust in our fellow man has slowly declined. Back in 1972, half of all Americans surveyed said they trusted each other. But now, 2/3rds of Americans surveyed say that "you can't be too careful" with people.

You'll find this to be very obvious in our political landscape. As April Clark, a political scientist and public opinion researcher from Purdue University, describes, *"It's like the rules of the game.* ***When trust is low, the way we react and behave with each other becomes less civil.****"*

Trust: The First Dysfunction

And, if you think this is getting better with the young people, think again. Pew Research shared their research on this very topic:

> *"Around three-quarters (73%) of U.S. adults under 30 believe people 'just look out for themselves' most of the time. A similar share **(71%) say most people 'would try to take advantage of you if they got a chance,'** and six-in-ten say most people 'can't be trusted.' Across all three of these questions, adults under 30 are significantly more likely than their older counterparts to take a pessimistic view of their fellow Americans."*

Most people would take advantage of you if you had the chance? That one caused me some shock. That means 7 out of 10 young people think that if given the opportunity to steal a valuable item from you, without consequences, they would. Sheesh…

Pew also reported that *"71% [of surveyors] think interpersonal confidence has worsened in the past 20 years."* The major cause according to the survey participants? **We're not as reliable as we used to be.** But, this caused me to think, did we really used to be more reliable 20 years ago? My parents seem to think so.

I gave them a quick call about this. Forty years ago, when they were in their twenties, they believed people to be much more honest. They discussed that there was a general adherence to a set of principles everyone collectively agreed with. It was much more habitual for people to attend church, so, because everyone did, there was a subconscious understanding of "right and wrong" (according to the Biblical definition of right and wrong). But, after 40 years of controversy, appalling acts of sin and major hypocrisy in church leadership and its attendees (not to mention other moments in history where Christians didn't act "Christ-like"), people questioned whether to still be part of Christianity. **Can we really trust this faith to be a reliable resource for life principles anymore?** Gallup poll research has shown a decline from 70% church attendance in 1999, to 50% church attendance in 2018. A sharp decline, indeed.

Without a central set of principles and beliefs that most Americans choose to follow, my parents discussed that people will do as the Bible professed in Judges 21:25, *"Everyone did what was right in his own eyes."* This creates tension, thereby creating distrust in each other. People start to ask each other skeptical questions like, "Why do you not believe what I believe? I believe I'm right. Why would you not agree?"

The response to this discourse in beliefs is to simply "coexist," but how real is this proclamation for peace? The very message that's preached to "coexist" creates tension with people who want to convert more people to their faith. **Any message by any leader creates tension because there will always be opposition.** Do you realize the President of the United States has never had a higher average voter approval rating than 70%?

That means there are still at least 30% of the population who want a new commander and chief at all times. As honest Abe Lincoln said in one of his famous speeches, *"A house divided against itself cannot stand."* This is actually based on scripture where Jesus first proclaimed, *"Every kingdom divided against itself is brought to desolation, and every city or house divided against itself will not stand. (Matthew 12:25)"* Since everyone continually gets fragmented with their own changing definitions of good and evil, there will be many more conflicts as we seek to make peaceful compromises.

Trust: The First Dysfunction

My parents also acknowledged that, with the internet, we have much quicker access to question the validity of statements. When someone claims something, it's now become instinctual for most to Google it prior to accepting the claim. Just think about how quickly reviews became a valid way to decide anything. According to BrightLocal, a search engine services company, 82% of consumers will read reviews before making a purchase decision. The average consumer will also read 10 reviews, and will often spend over 13 minutes vetting reviews and the product before making a purchase. **When we have access to so much fact checking, we have more to read about whether a product really is legit**. It's definitely better that we have this ability, but the consequence is we're now, culturally, way more skeptical about any claims, good or bad. **We're less trusting**.

So, if we can't trust people, who do we trust? Ourselves, I guess... that's at least the only person Glenn Villeneuve needed to trust.

Who's Glenn Villeneuve? This guy is an interesting fellow, because he deliberately chose to live in the wilderness. He's been a frequently featured subject on the show, *Life Below Zero*, lasting on the show for several seasons. It wasn't his motive to be on the big screen, but that came as a by-product of what he does. As a young man, he had a calling to live in nature, out in the wild. He talks about how, at thirteen years old, his mom just let him venture out into nature on a long walk through what's called The Long Trail, a 272 mile footpath going across the state of Vermont. He'd always been fascinated by nature and he asked himself a peculiar question. How could I actually make a life like this?

Pathetically Apathetic

Glenn Villeneuve carrying his next meal.

It doesn't get asked by many people today, but this man was devoted to this mission. In his mid-20's, he worked to build savings, cut off as many expenses as possible and spent several years learning what it takes to live and survive in the wilderness of Canada. He would learn answers to questions like: How do you fully utilize all the parts of an elk for survival? How do you best cook and use the bones, meat and even eyeballs for consumption? How do you keep warm in temperatures as low as 40 below zero? How do you prepare and stock meat for the winter? How do you add variety to your very limited diet in the wilderness?

During this time in the wilderness, he wanted to strip away everything he could depend on and simply depend on the land. He had no vehicles, a rifle, a frying pan, a pot, a self-built cabin and that's it. He didn't need anything else, and he was totally happy with that. He would walk at times for 20 to 25 miles just discovering what else he could find in the wild. It fascinated him to no end.

Trust: The First Dysfunction

As Joe Rogan interviewed Glenn on the *Joe Rogan Experience*, he's perplexed by Glenn's whole idea of living in the wild. Joe straight up asked him, *"Why is this life so appealing to you?"* And come on, I gotta ask the same question, too. Why would a man, in this day and age, decide to revert to how people lived before the Industrial Revolution?

Glenn responded by saying that he's in true harmony, peace and excitement when he lives in the wild. Back when he lived in a teepee in Vermont, he woke up with a smile on his face every day. He was excited about what was going on out there in the wilderness. He's "super fortunate," in his words, and realizes how few people get to have this experience.

This guy is literally trying to survive on a daily basis in the wilderness. No grocery stores, barely any internet, no heating and air conditioning, no plumbing systems…basically think of anything that comes automatic to how you live and he doesn't have that. Where would you get water if you didn't have grocery stores, water bottles available or running water in your home? **He can't trust that any of these basic amenities will be available.** He must kill the food and carry the food to camp and clean the food and cook the food and store the food for later. He not only needs to consider this for himself, but for his wife and three kids that would live with him in the wilderness!

Glenn can only trust in himself to make his survival happen, which was a very powerful appeal to him. He considers this to be one of the best aspects of living out in the wilderness in Canada. He doesn't rely on anything except his own aptitude to survive.

With Glenn living in the wilderness, he really only needs to figure out three things: gathering food, maintaining a great shelter and surviving. What do you think he doesn't need to rely on? He doesn't need to trust others to provide him food. He's got that. He doesn't need water filtration companies or sanitation companies to take care of his waste. He's got that. He doesn't need to trust that his 401k will actually do well enough to last him until retirement. Retirement wasn't a thing for Glenn during his time in the wilderness. No matter what happened, it's up to Glenn and that's it.

No one can take advantage of him because he's taking care of everything himself.

The appeal with Glenn Villeneuve is that he fended for himself and determined his own domain. He didn't need to rely on other parties to provide his survival. **That's why most of us find trust to be a challenging aspect of life. It requires other people, and other people have burned us plenty of times.** Other people flake out on social events, which makes the evening lame. They broke up with us and left us lonely, without love. They quit their job, which piled on more work for us. They didn't deliver on their end of the assignment and now the whole group fails because of it. And, whenever life seems to be working pretty well, someone comes along to break our trust. Isn't that how it usually goes?

But, let's remember the words of Kathryn from *The Five Dysfunctions of a Team*: **"Trust is the foundation of real teamwork."** Considering this, **we might argue that public trust should be the biggest problem of them all.** We can fantasize about a life like Glenn's; out on his own, fending for himself. But I doubt you'll be living in the wilderness anytime soon or decide to spend more than a decade preparing to live in the wild. That's how long it took for Glenn! **We must understand that Kathryn is right, trust is the foundation.**

Trust: The First Dysfunction

How Kathryn Built Trust in DecisionTech

How did Kathryn's adventures with DecisionTech go, anyway?

After her rousing speech about the importance of trust, she received initial pushback. Her team asked questions like, "Do you really know us that well? You've only just arrived at our company two months ago." There were other responses about how she doesn't have experience working in high tech culture, or that she just didn't understand how everyone typically worked. There were also complaints about meetings being too boring or that there wasn't enough time to focus on their "lack of trust."

See, this should be evidence enough that there were trust issues. Kathryn covers one recommendation for improving the team and the team reacts by leaping to criticism. They wouldn't even give Kathryn a chance to explain the steps or tell what the team needed to do to solve their trust issues. **If I may ask you immediately skeptical with people? Are you jumping to criticize and lament about a difficult topic? You likely have trust issues.**

Kathryn begins to implement steps to address the lack of trust with her team. **She first eliminates distractions.** She forces the team to take out any communications or electric devices from the meetings. Absolute focus must be necessary to address this issue.

Next, **she requests that the team open up the can of worms about their lives.** Oddly enough, the team at DecisionTech never got around to actually knowing each other on a personal level. So, Kathryn requested that the team spend just an hour talking about their lives and their backgrounds. What resulted from this simple task left people awestruck. As the book describes, *"It was really quite amazing.*

After just forty-five minutes of extremely mild personal disclosure, the team seemed tighter and more at ease with each other than at any time during the past year."

What was important for Kathryn was for the team to be open about good-natured, civil confrontation. There's a moment in the book where a team member is shown some honest criticism about her snarky attitude. After the team heard about each other's lives and stories, they were more comfortable to work as a team to address issues together. That was where Kathryn wanted the team.

She needed them to overcome the need for invulnerability. She needed them to eliminate their need to hold up a powerful facade. Remember from the Introduction how people have the Bias Blindspot? **By eliminating the tendency to think that we're always high and mighty, we're much more inclined to work together and build a trustworthy team.**

So, did the company improve after two years of work? Here's how the rest of the story goes:

- **There were four other dysfunctions that she addressed and solved with the team.** I'll give a brief statement about to teach.

- **Inattention to Results** - born out of a need to seek individual attention and acclaim at the expense of the team.

- **Fear of Conflict** - which creates artificial harmony, not true harmony. Kathryn levels with them by saying, *"I'd trade that false kind of harmony any day for a team's willingness to argue effectively about an issue and then walk away with no collateral damage."*

- **Lack of Commitment** - there isn't true buy-in with everyone in the team, creating weak, hesitant followers.

Trust: The First Dysfunction

- **Avoidance of Accountability -** by not holding each other accountable to what the agreed commitment was, drifting occurs and goals are not met.

- **Each of these areas are built on a foundation of trust.** A lack of trust in a team, according to Kathryn, must be solved before diving into any of these other issues. These issues are illustrated here:

- The team needed an additional company retreat to continue dedicated improvements and training on the five dysfunctions.

- Mikey, one of the senior team members, left the company during the 2nd company retreat. She did not like all the change that was occurring and actually left to work with a competitor.

- DecisionTech met their revenue goals three out of four quarters after Kathryn's involvement.

- Instead of the company being in 3rd place against their competitors, DecisionTech is now in a tie for 1st in market share.

- The overall morale of the company has dramatically increased and there's much less employee turnover. The team trusts in each other's commitment.

- The new team member to replace Mikey, Joseph, commented on the new team, two years after the 1st company retreat. This was his takeaway:

   "For the rest of the day they launched into some of the most passionate debates Joseph had ever heard and ended those debates with crystal-clear agreements and no sense of lingering bitterness. By the end of the session, Joseph decided he had joined one of the most unusual and intense executive teams he had ever seen, and he couldn't wait to become an active part of it."

How Trust Built 11 Championship Teams

This kind of teamwork illustrated in *The Five Dysfunctions of a Team* is put plainly by Phil Jackson as "The Circle of Love." It's the uniting alchemy which binds players and coaches together to project them towards a championship title ring. As a coach and player for eleven NBA championship teams for the New York Knicks, Chicago Bulls and Los Angeles Lakers, Phil Jackson describes eleven maxims of leadership in his #1 *New York Times* best-selling book, *Eleven Rings*. The first two maxims discuss management styles that contradict the norm, but massively reinforce trust in a group.

His first recommendation is to **lead from inside-out.** He felt it was more important to figure out how to position your team most effectively together, before trying to preach from "what the other competitors are doing." Each team is their own ecosystem and, while there are proven strategies, the team still needs to morph itself into a cohesive group. It's a repeated narrative throughout his book that **players need the freedom to position themselves to thrive on the team. They will always wait on you to save the day.**

In Jackson's famous "Triangle" system, the coach shares, *"you can't stand around and wait for the Michael Jordans and Kobe Bryants of the world to work their magic. **All five players must be fully engaged every second—or the whole system will fail.**"* If you haven't positioned yourself well into a helpful role for the team, you won't do well in this Triangle system. Phil Jackson knew that teams don't win championships if the team is just looking for the all-star to come in and save the game. This is exactly what one of Phil Jackson's mentors, Red Holzman (championship coach for the 1970 & 1973 New York Knicks), detailed during his time coaching. Red discusses:

> *"On a good team there are no superstars. There are great players who show they are great players by being able to play with others as a team. They have the ability to be superstars, but if they fit into a good team, they make sacrifices, they do things necessary to help the team win."*

The main lesson? **Don't lead as a dictator.** Allow people to step up, buy-in to the plan and trust in themselves and each other. Sure, you still must lead the charge because you are the leader, but **if you don't trust people to step up in responsibility, then you'll never have a winning team.**

Phil's second maxim on leadership emphasizes the importance of **"benching the personal ego."** You're hired to be the leader of your team's success. Oftentimes, as Jackson saw in his 33 years of coaching, this gave liberty for other coaches in the NBA to be the almighty dictator of the team. Or, because teams had star players and wild personalities, the coach was simply a people pleaser for his players.

Phil took a third approach. **He vouched for delegation and ownership of each person's role on the team**. Jackson writes:

> *"The most effective approach is to delegate authority as much as possible and to nurture everyone else's leadership skills as well. When I'm able to do that, it not only builds team unity and allows others to grow but also--paradoxically--strengthen my role as leader."*

By granting people the opportunity to claim their stake in the team's success, the leader receives buy-in from the players and staff, and the leader is respected in return for allowing this monitored freedom. **Ownership of each other's roles on the court helps ensure that everyone's got each other's backs.** This is even the case for off the court activities and responsibilities. Back in Phil Jackson's time playing in the NBA, he and his team members needed to wash their jerseys, personally. While some may loathe the necessity of doing this, Jackson's teammates on the New York Knicks found doing laundry a good tool to vet out bad fits for the team. Jackson writes:

> *"The old Knicks were used to taking responsibility for our own laundry because there was no equipment manager then, and strange as it may sound, washing our own uniforms had a unifying effect on the team.* **If the newcomers weren't willing to wash their own gear, we wondered whether they would take responsibility for what they had to do on court.***"*

Trust: The First Dysfunction

This goes back to Jackson's point on benching the personal ego. If you're too arrogant, spoiled and egotistical to simply wash your gear, how can you be trusted when it's four seconds on the clock and you need to make that pass to ensure a victory? **The lesson is to build up trust by relieving your own high and mighty mentality.**

What you may notice with both of these principles, is that **they work on an internal level.** By building trust in yourself and your role on the team, you build greater trust in the other team members. If everyone is doing a better job individually, then everyone can collectively trust each other to be more reliable.

The problem is that few people see trust in this way. Most people see trust as something you showcase for others. People see it as a transactional exchange. Since I scratched your back, now you need to scratch mine. You serve the customer, you help out a friend and they, in turn, need to trust you. **In most people's minds, trust is an outward, external expression, not internal.** And, the way most people are skeptical and untrustworthy of each other, it's going to take a lot to convince them you're trustworthy.

Where's the Proof?

This is why reviews and testimonials are becoming SO CRUCIAL to everything in life. When our world has provided us with so many bad stories and headlines, we now need more and more validation to prove our worth. We need clear evidence. We not only need it for one occasion, but we need it to happen several times. We not only need to see it several times, but we need to see that it works for years in a row.

Pathetically Apathetic

We need to know why it didn't work for some people, even when it worked for most people. We need proof. No puffery allowed!

This is the exact case for the consulting firm I work at. We had to grow our firm via massive cold calling. Our team members made a minimum of 150 to 200 calls per day, every day. We expanded to other marketing avenues, but this has been our bread and butter approach to our growth. Now, when I say cold calling, **these people have never heard our name before.** Right off the bat, these business owners associate anyone who calls them to "help grow their business" as a scammer. Even if the business owner did want to grow their business, they would want to know what we charge, why it works, how we can specifically help them, how we even got a hold of them in the first place, what other companies we've done work with and so on.

These business owners, especially long-term, small business owners, have been screwed before. Some other marketing company called them in the past. They decided to work with them and they signed a six-month contract. After the first month, they realized it was a waste of money and now, they are stuck with them for another five months. Then, they decided to reach out to a marketing firm in their local city. You can trust someone in your neighborhood, right? They gave them a chance, but that didn't work either. Then, they turn to a family member who knows some things about websites and marketing and social media. Nothing gets done there either. So, now our consulting company calls them saying that we can help. Why should they expect us to be any different?

We must show testimonials. Where do we go first for proof? We start by letting them know that our founder, Tim Redmond, grew his own company from scratch to $40 million per year in annual sales.

Trust: The First Dysfunction

Not only that, but he grew and managed a staff of over 350 employees. Growing a wildly successful company should be good enough right? Unfortunately, there are a lot of people who talk a big game about their past accomplishments, but haven't done anything in the last several years. **Where's the current proof?**

We also ask them to Google us and find our 350+ 5-star reviews from other business owners, friends and family members who love our work and our team. Not only that, but we ask them to watch an endless amount of testimonial videos from actual clients who have seen the fruits of our labor. In that first consultation with us, the business owner sees our proven systems, our specific steps, our real facts, case studies, and testimonials.

So, we have some tangible validation here...but what if it still doesn't work? Many of these small business owners are not making a ton of money and can't afford to spend thousands of dollars a month for a consulting and marketing team. To address this issue, we require no contracts. It's a month-to-month program, where you can "drop us like a bad habit." You also own all your marketing and website materials. We don't hold any of it hostage. On top of that, you get to name your price for the first month and it's a money-back guarantee.

But, we're just a company that's calling you on the phone. Want to see the evidence in person? We invite people to come see our offices by attending our 2-day business workshop. We're basically putting a years' worth of consulting into two packed days. We're providing all the facts and actual steps you need to implement successful growth for your business! Our business conferences are actually the highest and most reviewed business conferences in the world. Just search on Google "thrivetime show business conference" and you'll find thousands of people screaming our praises.

So, let's review…if you actually want to grow and improve your business, we give you hundreds of real testimonials, proven business systems that have worked in your industry and others, money-back guarantees, no contracts, marketing materials you keep and you even start at a discounted price for the 1st month. What else do you need!?

Even with all of this, people still think it's a scam. They still can't imagine it happening in their own lives. They believe the great testimonials and reviews are just something special that only happened with "those people." **They don't even bother to watch the reviews!**

The reality is, it's a much deeper issue that plagues these business owners. It's a bigger problem because, just like in the stories from Phil Jackson and Kathryn with DecisionTech, it's an internal problem. **These business owners no longer believe in themselves. They no longer trust themselves.**

The Biggest Betrayer of Our Trust? Ourselves.

There's a bigger crime that happens on a daily basis to everyone. It's not from the potential scammers out there who could take advantage of you. It's not from the lawmakers who won't keep their word. It's not from the car salesperson who's trying to get you to buy a car just so they get a commission. It's not from the shady big-time executive who lords over us with their stock options. **The biggest betrayer of our trust is ourselves.**

How do you communicate with yourself on a regular basis? It's commonly known as your "self-talk." The way my boss likes to put

Trust: The First Dysfunction

it, is by asking this question, **"If someone you met talked to you the way you talked to yourself, would you be friends with them?"** What I'm getting at here is **our self-talk and the commitments we make to ourselves matter more than anything else.** If we can't trust ourselves to make the right decisions or to follow through with our own commitments, why should we expect others to do the same?

This should remind you about our discussion early on in the book about The Bias Blindspot. We carry around with us a perception of reality that always looks to benefit us. What decisions will help us the most in life? How can every situation be made beneficial for us?

Let's just cut the crap here. 8% of people actually commit to New Years' Resolutions. 70% of employees do not like where they work. Over half the population is not engaged in their workplace and, furthermore, over half of Americans can't cover a surprise $500 expense. The life expectancy of Americans has declined for three years in a row and drug use has increased to an unprecedented level. Half of all marriages end in divorce and the most attended class in all universities is a psychology class at Stanford about finding happiness. **Does it really look like we're making good, committed decisions about our lives?**

COME ON. Let's just take an honest look at ourselves! How recently have you said you were going to do something, but then didn't do it? Even if it was just a small thing, like not working out...or sleeping in longer than you should...or deciding to just call a sick day because you're feeling bad...**it's all a lost sense of trust in ourselves.** After this happens once, then it happens again and again and again and then, whoops! Guess I won't be getting that flat stomach I always wanted! **Maybe next year...after six years of saying that it'll happen next year.**

Then it gets even worse because **after we consistently break the**

Pathetically Apathetic

trust with ourselves, we just give up. That's what happens with these business owners. Our consulting firm eagerly wants to help these people. We give them so many reasons to buy into our proven system, but they've already committed to it never working in the first place. **They settled for lackluster, which is the worst result of lost trust. They settled for a pathetically apathetic life.**

This is why trust is the first dysfunction. It's the biggest ingredient to solving our apathetic problems. We must put in the work, individually, to prove trustworthiness to ourselves. Then, as a result of our consistent ability to rely on our own word, others can actually rely on us. Now, everybody is benefiting and trusting each other more, because it all started with our ability to trust in ourselves. It takes the raw vulnerability that was pivotal for DecisionTech's turnaround. It takes a strong discipline to prove your role in the team, as Phil Jackson saw in his eleven championship teams.

A book I recommended you read in our first chapter was *How to Win Friends and Influence People*. The principles Dale Carnegie talks about are far from extraordinary. They are actually as easy as smiling more! Here are some of the basic lessons he recommends throughout the book:

- » Smile.
- » Don't criticize, condemn or complain.
- » Give honest and sincere appreciation.
- » Become genuinely interested in other people.
- » Be a good listener and encourage people to discuss further.
- » Talk to people in their interests, instead of purely talking about your interests. Make them feel important.
- » Show respect for the other person's opinions. Never just say, "You're wrong."
- » Don't call out people's mistakes in public, unless it's

Trust: The First Dysfunction

absolutely necessary. Allow the other person to save face.
» Acknowledge your mistakes before pointing the finger at someone else.

Really? A book that's sold over 30 million copies and all it talks about is smiling more?? There isn't some secret sauce that's been a "hidden treasure" to success? Then why are all these books telling us "if you do this one thing…if you buy into my program…if you do these three super moves…you will finally reach success?"

If you knew someone who (1) smiled a lot, (2) was genuinely interested in your interests, (3) gave you honest and sincere appreciation and (4) showed respect for your differing opinions, you would consider them your greatest friend in the whole wide world. You would confide all of your issues and plans and thoughts and dreams into this individual. You would invite them to every occasion. These signs of good character shown in *How to Win Friends and Influence People,* are signs of a trustworthy person.

We rarely know anyone like this because no one keeps it up. It's so much easier to think of ourselves. It's much more comfortable to blame and criticize others for our shortcomings. Honest, sincere appreciation? Why should I give it out when no one has given it to me? **We're waiting so long for trustworthy people to be in our lives when, in reality, we are the who need to show up.**

If we never take the intensity to prove our own trustworthiness… if we never get obsessed about standing by our word… even when our word is just with ourselves… then, why bother? Why try to care or try to make things better, when we can't trust that it will ever get better?

Pathetically Apathetic

Take the lessons from Kathryn in *Five Dysfunctions of a Team*. ***"The fact is, if we don't trust one another—and it seems to me that we don't—then we cannot be the kind of team that ultimately achieves results."***

Take the lessons from Phil Jackson in *Eleven Rings*. ***"It's a mysterious juggling act that requires not only a thorough knowledge of the time-honored laws of the game but also an open heart, a clear mind and a deep curiosity about the ways of the human spirit."***

Take the lessons from Jesus Christ, for Christ's sake! ***"Every kingdom divided against itself is brought to desolation, and every city or house divided against itself will not stand."***

2/3rds of Americans don't trust each other, but we can't even trust ourselves. By fostering a committed trustworthiness to yourself, more people will trust you. More people can rely on you to be a non-apathetic human being. Then everyone collectively becomes more awesome.

Trust is the first dysfunction.

Trust: The First Dysfunction

CHAPTER 4:

The Enormous Problem With Saving the World

Would you like to save the world?

I attended college at Oral Roberts University in Tulsa, Oklahoma. It's a private Christian college that's consistently ranked in the top three worst party schools in America. To the college, that's a statistic of pride. They wear that badge with honor and, each year, the president will remind the student body that the college is dead last in party schools. So, as you might assume, I don't have any raging party stories to tell you about from college. I'll happily listen and laugh about yours all night long though.

Since it's a Christian college, we held chapel sessions. It's basically a church service the campus holds for us every single week. A worship band sings songs and then, the President or a guest speaker will preach a sermon. At the end of most chapel services, there will likely be a huge call for us to go out and change the world. This is based on a Biblical reference in the book of Matthew about The Great Commission where it says, *"Therefore go and make disciples of all nations, baptizing them in the name of the Father and of the Son and of the Holy Spirit, and teaching them to obey everything I have commanded you.* (Matthew 28:19-20)"

It's also based on the vision statement that's posted on the back of the ORU chapel building. The story goes that Oral Roberts (the founder of the school), was sitting in a cafeteria and God gave him a command about the new university he was building. His command was to, *"Raise up your students to hear My voice, to go where My light is dim, where My voice is heard small, and My healing power is not known, even to the uttermost bounds of the earth. Their work will exceed yours, and in this I am well pleased."* This was God's commission to Oral Roberts for his university.

To Oral Roberts' credit, he achieved the dream. He built one of the most prominent Christian universities the world has ever known. The campus represents 115 countries, and that's remarkable considering there are only about 4,100 students that attend the college at any given time. In 2017, 568 of those students participated in trips around the world to serve impoverished communities in the United States, and around the globe. That means approximately 14% of the college raised hundreds of thousands of dollars on their own to go out and make an impact in the world. With many alumni like Jim Stovall, Bill Weir, Ryan Tedder and Joel Osteen, the students are an interesting bunch.

But, at the end of each chapel service, the President, or one of the speakers, will likely make a decree to go out and CHANGE YOUR WORLD! "God spoke us into existence for a purpose and a calling. Go out with the gifts you have and be an example for God's Kingdom. GO OUT THERE AND MAKE A DIFFERENCE! MAKE THE WORLD A BETTER PLACE!"

Whether you profess to be a Christian or not, you've undoubtedly heard this same message. You hear it from our elected presidents, our government leaders, our philanthropic business owners, our motivational speakers, our church pastors and anybody who's looking to stir up a crowd. It's the basis for many motivational seminars and talks. GET OUT THERE AND SEIZE YOUR FUTURE! YOU ARE

Pathetically Apathetic

SPECIAL THE WAY YOU ARE. NOW GO BE AWESOME! You're amped up and everyone is cheering around you. It's a great collective feeling, similar to screaming for your favorite band or watching your favorite sports team win the game. The energy is palpable. You can feel it in the air. You walk away feeling like a champ!

It's only for a brief moment, though. So, after that rip-roaring Sunday sermon to radically transform your world, you get out of the auditorium and head to the car. You're still feeling awesome and you're chatting with your wife about how good today's service was. Suddenly, as you drive back home, someone cuts you off on the road and a curse word slips out. Your kids are in the back and they ask you, "What does *fuck* mean?" You explain that it's a naughty word and you shouldn't say it. Ugh, that's not a good moment for your parenting.

Then, you think about your day and realize that it's your cousin's birthday party today and you didn't want to go. You have to go, though, because he would notice and things would get awkward. But, wait...YOU HAVEN'T GOTTEN HIM A GIFT! Detour! It's time to run to Target. You pick up impulse groceries and some stupid gift and head back home. As you finally arrive home, you turn on some Sunday football to kick back and relax. You probably took a nap and your wife woke you up to get ready for the birthday party you don't care about. Then, you innocently check your email and realize that you didn't respond to an important one from work. You need to say something intelligent before Monday morning rolls around. It's also about that one client who's constantly on your ass about unimportant matters, so you really don't want to respond. Now that you're thinking about emails, you think about Monday morning and all the stresses that come with it.

The Enormous Problem With Saving the World

Suddenly, in the span of just a couple hours, life got incredibly normal again. The inspiring message to go and change your world is long gone. What happened to that motivation?

What just happened, happens every Sunday morning for a majority of the church-going population. It also happens to everyone who attends a lively business conference. It happens to people who watch an impactful movie at the theater or finish reading a deep and meaningful book (like this one). It's a key warning that's given to Christians in the Bible, but can also be applied to any well-meaning individual. "*But be doers of the word, and not hearers only, deceiving yourselves.* (James 1:22)."

What just happened is you heard a great message to go and make an impact, with no roadmap on how to actually do it.

It's not entirely your fault. Most messages from a pulpit or a stage aren't very practical. You weren't clearly told what to do in order to solve the world's problems or change your life. You were given a vague concept that sounded great, but doesn't give you any serious tools to work with. So, even if you did try to figure out how to make an impact, you wouldn't get very far.

You were told to GET OUT THERE and CHANGE YOUR WORLD, right? **But what the hell does that even mean?** This is too complicated to think about, so you continue to stress about your current problems. The overdue bills, the car that's got a couple dents you want to fix, the apartment that's seen better days, the clothes you needed to wash yesterday, the problem child you can't seem to make better...and there go all those problems in the world. **All the problems we were told to solve, magically floated away into the breeze.**

It's awesome that so many people maintain a dreamy-eyed vision about their future. They want to get out there to become doctors, create non-profit organizations, pass the bar exam to defend the innocent and make the world a better place. Who doesn't want to be a positive influence? **We must realize, though, that saving the world isn't a momentary decision**. It's not a one-time, flip the switch situation. Before any of the real world-changers started building orphanages in South America, or built their thriving nonprofits to bring people off of drug addiction, or provided tons of money to impoverished families in their city, they all did something very important.

They all started by saving *their* world and themselves. As these world changers took small, humble steps to help improve their close surroundings, their realm of influence expanded further. And, now, after decades of being a great human to society, they created a thriving life for themselves, helping many others thrive. People finally come up to them after a decade and ask, "Man, how did you do it? I want to do what you do!"

What these spectators don't realize is **it's absolutely unrealistic to think we can solve giant problems without investing several years to improve ourselves and the world within our reach.** It's a humbling first few years for these great individuals, but the decades afterwards will look quite heroic. I believe a great example of this can be found in Andrew Carnegie's life. You may believe he's a man who had all the right things occur, but I'd argue that **even the most privileged of people can squander their opportunities instead of seize them.** Let's see how Mr. Carnegie saved this world bank in the late 1800s.

The Enormous Problem With Saving the World

How One Man Saved His World

Andrew Carnegie was the steel magnate in the late 1800s, and was considered one of America's wealthiest individuals. Andrew Carnegie's steel company in 1901, was the first company valued at $1 billion (this is also valued in 1901 money, so we're talking about a $29 billion company in today's money). In 1901, he sold his steel company to J.P. Morgan for what would equate to approximately $401 billion in 2019. What did Carnegie do with his wealth? He is well-known for his philanthropy, where he would invest his wealth into libraries, museums, performance arts centers and other hallmark places in the United States. You can't deny that Andrew Carnegie's philanthropic efforts created a ripple effect of positivity in countless lives. **Andrew Carnegie is no apathetic man.**

Andrew Carnegie had a rough childhood, though. He started working as young as 12 years old for only about $35/week in today's dollars. He was working in a cotton mill for 12 hours a day, 6 days per week. His parents weren't wealthy, either. They tried and tried to sell garments and crops, but his father was never able to maintain himself as the breadwinner of the house. In those early years for Carnegie, **there was one blessing given to him that granted him the opportunity to become one of the wealthiest individuals in America: philanthropy.**

That's right. The only reason he had the opportunity to be educated was due to the Free School of Dunfermline. This school was gifted to the town Carnegie grew up in by Adam Roland, a prominent judge in Scotland at the time. It was because of this charitable act that Carnegie was able to start his education and become a heavy reader. In fact, while he worked in his labor-intensive jobs, he was so well-known to be an avid reader that James Anderson, a colonel in Pennsylvania opened up his 400 volume personal library to Carnegie each Saturday evening.

Pathetically Apathetic

Carnegie kept digesting knowledge as quickly as he could and kept working hard in his job. Soon enough, he would be steadily promoted to new positions of income and responsibility.

He started working for only $1.20/week ($35 in 2019 money). Then he would move to a very strenuous job at $2.00/week ($59 in 2019). After working in labor-intensive production plants for years, he would move to working as a messenger and telegraph boy at $2.50/week ($77 in 2019). Then, at 18 years old, he would work for the Pennsylvania Railroad Company for $4.00/week ($123 in 2019). This company was in a growing industry, where Carnegie saw more prospects for a career. On top of this, the Pennsylvania Railroad Company was one of the largest companies in railroad work. For six years, he diligently continued this work, until he was given responsibility over a division of the company, which propelled him to earn a salary of approximately $1500/year ($43,000/year in 2019). Steadily and surely, he would continue to advance in his discipline, wealth and opportunities, to later own the Keystone Bridge Company and ride the wave of the great Industrial Revolution. The rest is history.

We could continue down his biography, but what I care about is the beginning stages of development. Did you notice something about his early years? There's a trend you'll find that's very important for anyone who wants to save the world. **Carnegie worked his ass off.** He worked for 6 days per week continually for several years, starting at 12 years old. It took Andrew Carnegie nine years of this intensive labor to advance from hell jobs to managerial responsibilities, where he earned a decent living. And, because he developed this intense work ethic, it became easier for him to continue to work hard and take more responsibility. His realm of influence could successfully expand because he consistently proved his worth in the earlier years. He developed a dominant work ethic that very few could match.

The Enormous Problem With Saving the World

But, it wasn't simply working hard that got him to the top. Lots of people work hard. Lots of people slave day-in and day-out at their jobs and never seem to advance to better opportunities. **Andrew Carnegie treasured his education and continued to build up the bottomless chest of wisdom.** This is also important when trying to save the world. He started with free education in his hometown in Scotland, but he didn't settle for that. He read whatever he could, and continued to advance with his personal education. Because of this, his intellect expanded and gave him the insights and aptitude to make wise decisions about his future. He knew that moving to the railroad industry would lead him to more prospects for a wealthier career than working as a telegrapher would. He didn't just work harder and expect to be "rewarded" for showing up. **He actively sought opportunity.** If we want to solve problems in our world, we must actively seek opportunities to do so, instead of purely staying in our comfortable lane.

That's a third aspect of Carnegie's ability to grow wealth. As a telegrapher, **he kept up with who the influential people were** in his town in Pennsylvania. He fastidiously continued to maintain connections with these wealthy individuals. It was because of this that he found the opportunity to receive 400 volumes of education for free from Colonel James Anderson. Later in his career, because of his employment and consistent success at the Pennsylvania Railroad Company, Carnegie would stay connected to his wealthy bosses (Thomas A. Scott and John Edgar Thomson) for them to invest in multiple companies that Carnegie would establish. The only reason those two men would be willing to associate with Carnegie is due to his discipline, hard work, intellect and continued success as their employee at the Pennsylvania Railroad Company.

Pathetically Apathetic

At 24 years old, Carnegie was given responsibility for an entire division of the Pennsylvania Railroad Company, which at the time was one of the first big businesses in the United States. Think about yourself at 24 years old...how successful do you think you would be in this position? Could you manage an entire division of one of the largest companies in the United States at the time? I couldn't even manage my own dishes!

It was because of these intense years of developed intellect and pursuit that he was able to become a huge philanthropist, himself! Historical records show that during his last 18 years of life, he donated over $350 million (in 2019, this would conservatively be $65 billion), to organizations that would revolutionize how Americans develop and expand their knowledge. With reading alone, he built 3,000 different libraries, and is the very reason why libraries are so prominent in our country. Up until just the past several years, people were using these libraries as their main source of accumulating knowledge. **Can you imagine how many lives Carnegie has been able to help just by granting people free access to all of these libraries?** That's what you call saving the world.

Did Andrew Carnegie have troubles in his business? Yes. Did Carnegie have employees who hated him or thought he worked them too hard? Yes. In fact, on more than a couple occasions, there were worker strikes that took place within his companies. With any business leader or anyone who aggressively pursues a goal, there will be enemies and adversaries. But, Carnegie explains in his book, *Gospel of Wealth,* why the accumulation of wealth is helpful and important for contributing to society, and saving the world. He writes,

The Enormous Problem With Saving the World

*"This, then, is held to be the duty of the man of wealth: To set an example of modest, unostentatious living, shunning display or extravagance; to provide moderately for the legitimate wants of those dependent upon him; and, after doing so, to consider all surplus revenues...to administer in the manner which, in his judgment, is best calculated to produce the most beneficial results for the community—**the man of wealth thus becoming the mere trustee and agent for this poorer brethren, bringing to their service his superior wisdom, experience and ability to administer, doing for them better than they would or could do for themselves."***

There's a Reason Why Heroes Are Heroes

Carnegie was a young kid who worked harder than anyone else, studied harder than anyone else and worked valuable connections better than anyone else, **in an obsessive pursuit of excellence.** There's a burning fire passion, or a "dragon energy," as one of my bosses calls it, to not settle for poverty any longer. He saw any opportunity that was worthwhile and attacked it at full force. He spent years upon years doing this. You could say that this was just the way he lived his life.

Now, you may look at a guy like Andrew Carnegie and say, "This is a once in a lifetime kind of man. You expect me to become Andrew Carnegie?" You're missing the point here. I don't care about what kind of end-goals you have in mind. **I care about the character traits and attitudes that you find in everyone who makes a difference, no matter how large the impact may be.** Whether it's someone who owns a local mom and pop bakery or someone who's a hedge fund manager, we all can still save our worlds.

Pathetically Apathetic

• • • •

But, let's just think, how do most people in their early years and 20-somethings live their life? There are obvious stereotypes that we could speculate about. Who cares about stereotypes and speculations, though? We want to know facts!

Well, the Bureau of Labor Statistics actually put together demographic research on the average 29 year-old. The quotes I'm pulling are from a piece done by *The Atlantic*. Here's their conclusion on what the average 29 year-old looks like:

> *"The average 29-year-old did not graduate from a four-year university, but she did start college; held several jobs, including more than two in the last three years; is not as likely to be married as her parents at this age, but is still likely to be living with somebody; is less likely to own a home than 15 years ago."*

Let's go through some of the researched facts, and pick out some key insights.

Education: *"The average 29-year-old did not graduate from a four-year university, but she did start college."*

There's a growing number of people who started to gain an education past high school, but failed to complete the education. It's even worse for black and Hispanic communities, where four out of five college attendees didn't finish college. White kids have better statistics, but still, only one out of three Caucasian students finish their degrees.

Work: *"held several jobs, including more than two in the last three years…"*

The Enormous Problem With Saving the World

Work is very non-committal these days. The former fantasy of finding a great company and sticking with them for decades practically doesn't exist with these 29 year-olds. The majority of them have held more than seven jobs prior to turning 29. On top of that, in the past couple years of their life (25 - 28 years old), the average 29 year-old held more than two jobs. **Now, what about kids who dropped out of high school? It's quite rough, with the typical 18 to 28 year-old only holding a job for approximately six months.** In the same research, it's also cited that the typical annual salary for 29 year-olds is $35,000.

Marriage: *"is not as likely to be married as her parents at this age, but is still likely to be living with somebody..."*

Married folks with kids are on a steep decline. In 1960, 84% of people from 25 to 29 years old would be married. In 2010? Only 42% are married. This doesn't really mean that we're suddenly without love. While it's obvious that these 29 year-olds are slow to marry, 60% are either married, living with a partner or cohabiting together. So, it seems that, due to the vast number of marriages that end in divorce, more and more people are becoming skeptical of marriage. More and more people are becoming less trusting to commit for the long haul.

Living: *"is less likely to own a home than 15 years ago."*

Homeownership for every age demographic is in decline. While, 15 years ago, 44% of 29 year-olds owned a home, only 35% of them now own a home. There's a good percentage of these 29 year-olds that are finding homes on the outskirts of cities and suburbs, too, because of skyrocketing home prices within cities. This also creates heavier traffic times, lost earning potential and lost sleep. According to a 2009 study on sleep duration, the percentage of people sleeping less than six hours per day has increased while sleeping more than 8 hours per day has declined.

• • • •

Does the average 29 year-old look like someone who's on course to positively influence their world? Do you expect these 29 year-olds to blaze a trail that's going to positively impact people's lives? It doesn't seem like it, according to the research above.

Now, I know that, as I ask these questions, doubters and haters will be quick to jump on me. Are there plenty of reasons and excuses for why the United States economic system and social environment could negatively affect people's livelihoods? Yes. Again, we're missing the point. There are clear differences between people who live apathetic lives and people who live non-apathetic lives. You'll find over and over again that people who solve large-scale issues in the world are not normal people, and have rarely acted like normal people. **The remarkable people are remarkable, because they don't do what everyone else is doing.**

I guess that's why heroes are heroes. Andrew Carnegie worked feverishly, for his entire life, to spend his last 18 years playing the role of the hero. You can't ignore the fact that tens of thousands of employees can thank him for the jobs they had.

Bill Gates followed a similar story. For decades, he worked and worked to build up Microsoft to the powerhouse that it is. Because of this dedication, we're seeing in real-time his foundation, the Bill & Melinda Gates Foundation, making total grant payments of $50 billion over the lifetime of the foundation. It took Justin Wren several years, since 2013, to say that he's built over 100 wells in the Congo and Uganda. But, remember how, in chapter 1, we saw how much

The Enormous Problem With Saving the World

Justin Wren needed to change his life? He also couldn't have provided these Pygmy people with the resources they needed without his years of training and dominance as a fighter in the UFC. How else could you explain his ability to build and fund over 100 wells in less than a decade? Justin Wren needed his skills in wrestling and his inspiring comeback story to take place prior to saving the Pygmy people.

No matter what opportunities these people did or didn't have, they still chose to consistently be above average. They chose to take on the role of influencer. They made conscious decision after conscious decision to keep saying "yes" to the challenge. They never settled for average. They put in the many, many hours of effort required to become remarkable and impactful.

In fact, there's a theory that's been immensely studied called the "10,000 Hour Rule." The theory purports it's estimated that it takes at least 10,000 hours of work to master anything. Daniel Levitin, neurologist and author of four consecutive #1 best-selling books, discusses how pivotal this rule is to fostering excellence in any area:

> *"In study after study, of composers, basketball players, fiction writers, ice skaters, concert pianists, chess players, master criminals, and what have you, this number comes up again and again. Of course, this doesn't address why some people get more out of their practice sessions than others do.* ***But no one has yet found a case in which true world-class expertise was accomplished in less time. It seems that it takes the brain this long to assimilate all that it needs to know to achieve true mastery.***"

In order for us to save the world, we must prove ourselves, over time, to be the worthy heroes. Saviors and heroes do not live average lives for a reason. This is why it's erroneous to expect ourselves to be heroes overnight!

We've already talked, at length, about how people can't seem to trust each other, hindering their faith in humanity, and themselves. As for this chapter, I'd like to ask this main question: **If we look at our own lives, how should we expect ourselves to start saving the world?** How can my fellow college students at Oral Roberts University expect to go out there and "change the world" when we've been so unremarkable? When we continue to be so average in our time and efforts, how can we expect results that are above average?

Here's the good news…**we can save the world, or rather, save *our* world.**

How to Save Our World

We all live in our own bubble of society, right? We interact with our own friends, family members, work colleagues and other humans. **How are we a hero to them?** Being a good friend to a person who needs it? Doing an extra call after hours with a customer or client to make their day? Sending someone a gift they didn't expect? Calling your grandpa after so many months of little communication? **These are all ways to save *our* world.**

Could you be as fantastical as these giant tycoons? Of course! You could spend your entire life focused on the kind of pursuits that these lovely individuals have done. You could be a great blessing to a large majority of the population with your big contribution. **But will you? And, will it really ruin your life if you aren't the gigantic hero you dream of?** Maybe just being a better than average citizen of the world,

The Enormous Problem With Saving the World

who's thoughtful and caring of those around them is enough. It's more than enough for most people, because, as you can see, **we all simply need a little better than average from each other.**

We can save *our* world quite effectively and realistically, and that ambition will be just as important as the Andrew Carnegies of our time. What does your pathway look like to save *your* world?

First and foremost, **it starts with saving yourself.** You'll continue to read and find out in this book that I'm a HUGE advocate for self-improvement. You are not a useful human being to the world if you (1) can't get your life together and independently support yourself, (2) can't find a cause or means to improve the world around you or (3) can't live a positive and encouraging life to others and yourself. You may be suffering through your finances, depending on the government for aid and solely focused on getting yourself out of your poverty hole, but at least you are trying. **If you aren't taking the effort to save yourself, don't expect to save others around you.**

Next, **assist the lowest hanging fruit around you.** While there are drastic problems around the world, there are also suffering people in your local area. Friends, family members and work colleagues need good people too. **Be a positive influence to those currently around you.**

Finally, **prove through consistency your worth.** Prove that you can transform *your* world, wherever your circle of influence is. If you feel called to jump ship and be a source of light to a far-off land, be my guest! You are an awesome person for caring about those lost and hurting people. **It just doesn't do you or anyone any good if your efforts are wasted by your own dysfunction.**

What if we decided to take small steps to improve our own lives before we became keyboard warriors and critiqued our politicians?

How much better could the world be if we decided to, instead of saving the world, start by saving ourselves? As a result, you actually WILL be saving the world. You'll be ridding the world of another average, unremarkable person.

Then, if you wanted to go after the large-scale world problems, how much more equipped would you be? You just spent years fostering an improved lifestyle where you can handle so much more. So, why not tackle bigger problems? You've been doing a great job solving the problems in your life and in the lives of those you're surrounded by.

That sounds admirable enough to me. How about you?

The Enormous Problem With Saving the World

CHAPTER 5:

Obsession is Weird

"I no longer listen to what people say. I just watch what people do."
- ANDREW CARNEGIE

Calendars are brutally honest. I didn't use one for a majority of my life, because I'm only 25 years old and most 20-somethings can't even hold a job, let alone a calendar. Here's the kind of guy I was: I was the guy who did as much as he needed to in order to get acceptable, respectable recognition. That meant I was a B+ to A- student. Sometimes, I'd get an awesome grade, and, sometimes, I'd get a horrible grade. My philosophy was to study hard enough to get better than average grades, and don't work any harder than that. Because, why should I? I was still doing well right?

This translated into most other areas of my life growing up. For instance, did you ever need to mow the lawn growing up? Get out in the hot sun, flare up your allergies in the grassy backyard and earn no pay? Or how about doing your own laundry? It's a pretty simple task, but so simple that it's easily forgettable. How about cleaning your room? Or even the entire house? Did the parents reprimand you for leaving your room looking like a nuke exploded?

Obsession is Weird

See, none of that happened with me. I've never mowed a lawn in my life. I also rarely ever cleaned dishes, did yard work in my mom's garden, swept the house or really anything responsible for taking care of a home. I did my own laundry, but it was always last minute and I never cleaned my room until guests were coming, and only after frequent commands from my mother.

In relationships, I didn't try hard at all, because, why should I? I found girls attractive, but I saw the dating activities, the cute things that couples do and the constant "sweetness" as kind of annoying, honestly. In working jobs, I would start a job and work for only three to six months, because the job would start to get annoying. I didn't need a job either, so why continue to be annoyed? In my physical fitness, I participated in sports, but I didn't care about being the absolute best in the sport. I would've liked to be great, but the dedication that's required looked intimidating.

I didn't try hard in life, because I didn't need to...which, unbeknownst to me, caused a giant obstacle to take shape in my life. It caused me to leave college with no career path or direction, which led me to believe college was a waste. In the first six months after college, I got depressed and felt the world just pass me by. When I worked a job I didn't like, at home all day with no friends to comfort me, with an immense lack of clarity in life, it shouldn't be so surprising that I was depressed. **I suffered from deep seated apathy, without knowing it.**

What I didn't realize is that I lacked an immensely important character trait that's found in anyone who makes anything significant out of their lives. The successful millionaires and billionaires in business, the acclaimed actors in movies and television, the musicians who are more than a one-hit wonder, the athletes who not only stay in the professional leagues, but thrive in their sports, and any other person in your life who's an outstanding citizen...**every single one of these stars had an obsession with their particular skill.**

We can all become consumed by tasks from time to time. That's not unique. **These folks were continually obsessed with their one skill.** Every single one of the greats spent a lifetime achieving dominance step-by-step. They sacrificed huge amounts of their "average childhood" to excel at a young age. The word "obsession" isn't a stretch either. Actors can always be found watching movies, going through scripts, finding all sorts of opportunities to act and work on their own material. Tom Cruise, arguably one of the best action stars of our time, has publicly stated that he watches a movie every single day, no matter what.

Athletes all started with a knack for the sport, but the great ones were obsessed with it. While most kids who played tennis only practiced a couple times per week, because it was fun, the great ones worked out in the mornings before school, played for three hours after school and did the same thing every day for a decade. The great ones watched tennis matches of Roger Federer, Serena Williams, Maria Sharapova and Rafael Nadal all the time. They would dedicate their time to, not only watch for enjoyment, but to take notes and practice what the great ones were doing. They would film themselves and critique each movement in their game. They would actively participate in tournaments and, likely, do nothing else with their lives except school, tennis and sleep.

All of these polarizing figures in our lifetime said this at one point: "You know what...I can make something out of this skill. I'm pretty good at it and I'd like to give it my all! I'm going to remove any alternative options and commit to making it in _____ (fill in the blank). If I fail? Well, at least I'll have found something better or I'll have died trying."

Obsession is Weird

They talked about being one of the best, and they meant it. They walked the talk better than all of their peers who also wanted to be the best. Elon Musk, the real life Tony Stark, talks about this kind of dedication and hard work. Elon instructs:

> *"Work like hell. I mean you just have to put in 80 to 100 hour weeks every week. [This] improves the odds of success. If other people are putting in 40 hour work weeks and you're putting in 100 hour work weeks, then even if you're doing the same thing you know that you will achieve in 4 months what it takes them a year to achieve."*

Expectations vs. Reality

You are not Elon Musk, though. You didn't come to the United States as an immigrant, work in life-threatening jobs, frequently pull all-nighters and have the discipline to work your ass off ingrained in you. You don't have the mindset that's birthed from great poverty and life challenges, to propel you to create more than four of the most innovative companies to date (Paypal, Tesla, SpaceX, SolarCity, etc.). Oh yeah, he's also not even 50 years old.

I don't know who you are or what you've done with your life so far, but my best guess is that if you picked up a book titled, *Pathetically Apathetic*, you are likely reading or listening to improve your life. While there are lots of amazing self-help books out there, you decided that the word *apathy* struck a chord with you.

But, to be honest, your life probably isn't that terrible. I'm making assumptions, but go with me here...you're able to hold up a job (barely). You may be late in one or two bills, but you're not bankrupt or on the streets. You have a family, but, if you're honest, you've got a problem child, and if your spouse does that one thing ONE MORE TIME, I SWEAR…it's not the "ideal" circumstances, but it's not terrible. Give yourself a pat on the back for once! Honest to God, you aren't a complete failure!

You could be doing pretty decently for yourself! You could be reading this book while just receiving an awesome raise or a sweet new position in a hot company. You could be in a new relationship with someone way out of your league. You could be financially healthy and that's pretty cool, because only 29% of Americans in 2019, would consider themselves to be savvy with their money. **But, like me, you always looked at making your life remarkable, and you're not really sure what that means.** There's this lingering thought that things could be better.

Whether good, bad or whatever the case, the way you are living right now likely isn't the dream life you envisioned growing up. There's usually a harsh reality everyone faces at some point in their "coming of age," where expectations abruptly clash with reality. You get into the first great job in your field and quickly realize what it takes to make the big bucks. You started online dating because nothing else is producing great results and, after a couple meetups in person, you quickly find out how deceiving those photos are.

That's why the Expectations vs. Reality memes are so popular (see images on page 100).

Memes help bring out the fantasies we have about ourselves and dramatically illustrate the reality of how we truly act. It gives us a very clear look at how the feelings we have are so, *SO* optimistic.

When I wear a tight shirt

How I feel   How I look

HOW I THINK I LOOK   HOW I ACTUALLY LOOK

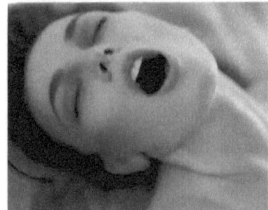

Pathetically Apathetic

There's always someone you know trying to improve their physique, right? When you ask them at the start, they say, "Oh yeah! Me and my friend are totally going to start running outside on that trail. It's pretty and we're keeping each other accountable to our commitment." The next day they say, "Eww it's raining, let's wait until tomorrow." Next week?..."You know, things have just gotten really busy, but don't worry, we're still going to start running." Yeah, I don't believe that for a second.

The Expectations vs. Reality meme hits home on one of the clearest psychological findings out there. It's what psychologists call our self-serving bias. **With the self-serving bias, we distort circumstances in order to maintain and enhance our self-esteem.** We tend to perceive ourselves in an overly-pleasing or favorable manner. We see ourselves as way better than what we really are. In order to keep sane during our up-and-down lives, we always take a justified spin on our actions...or, rather, our lack of action.

A phenomenal series of books on our inclination to self-justify our actions was done by The Arbinger Institute. In their first book of the series titled *Leadership & Self-Deception*, they teach us about being "in the box" and "out of the box" with our communication. Other leadership books phrase the concept differently, but the premise goes like this...we all live in our self-perceived reality. Since we are typically the most popular person to ourselves, we view the world in a way that benefits us the most and we make decisions based on giving ourselves the best benefits.

Obsession is Weird

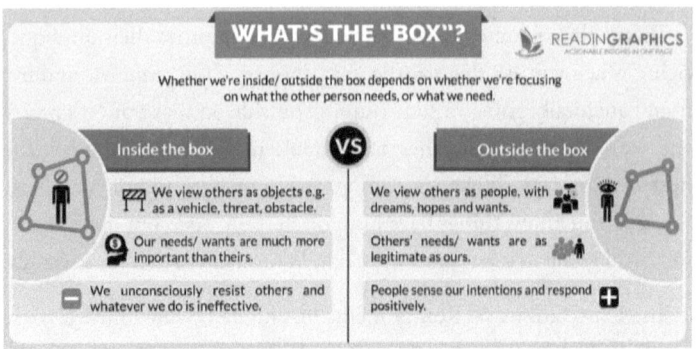

(An infographic to help communicate the ideas of "the box")

Unfortunately, this breeds very poor communication skills and easily forms corrupted work environments. If everyone thinks and lives in their "box of reality," if everyone talks from within the box, then they eliminate their ability to get out of their box and truly understand what others are communicating. **We ignore the humanity in others by speaking to them from inside our box.** If we, first, remove ourselves from the box and our own self-deceptions of reality, then we can truly correct and make improvements.

If we can't be honest with ourselves, we'll continually make excuses for why things aren't as awesome as they "should" be. The expectations will always negatively interact with our reality. This is why truly excellent environments often bring a great reality check.

Pathetically Apathetic

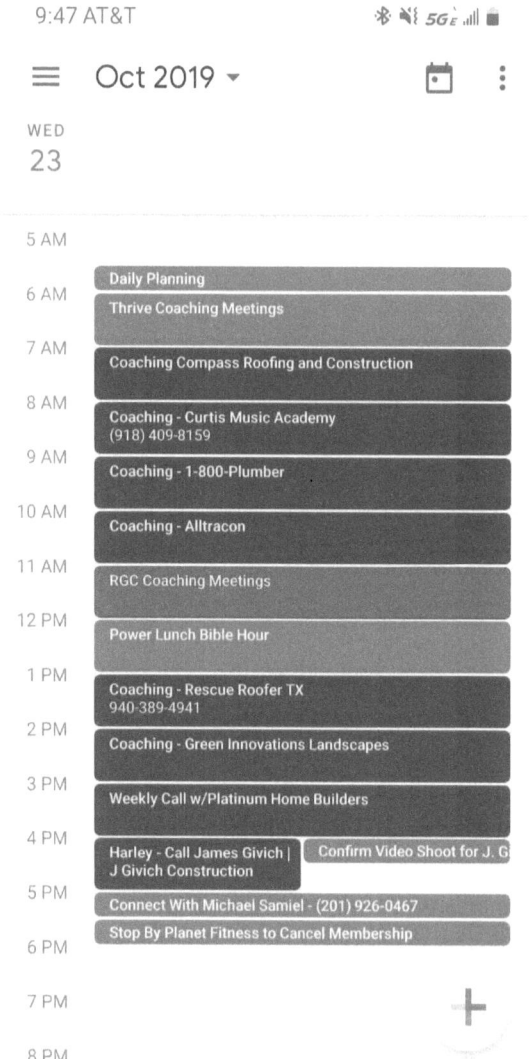

(What's not included is the 4:30 am alarm to get to work by 5:30 am)

Excellence is Shocking

> *"Some people aren't used to an environment where excellence is expected."*
>
> - Steve Jobs

In the first week of work at the consulting firm after college, I did not know how to handle it.

People were so focused on providing excellence at every level. Everyone has key performance indicators (goals, numbers, sales, etc.) to hit every single day with their job. If they miss the mark for one day, they would be confronted and advised to hit the goal. Miss the mark two times? You're takin' a ride into the danger zone!

Everyone carries around a to-do list, and often adds more than four or five additional items throughout the day. Everyone creates calendars for themselves to manage their time and plan their day, (see page 103 for a screenshot of a typical scheduled day). They actually show up to work early to put together their calendar and to-do list for each day. These aren't just vague calendars with one or two reminders, either. These people literally block out their entire day. Just take a look at my calendar for what a typical day looks like.

Everyone is always doing something that involves work. Break rooms? HA! That does not exist, since it's an open space office. No one took breaks except to eat lunch, which, half the time, was spent staying productive. I swear we should be sponsored by BANG energy drinks, due to the amount of cans we throw down each day. I'm sure many of us will have long-term negative effects on our health because of the energy drinks and multiple cups of coffee we consume.

Pathetically Apathetic

Everyone works in the same mindset at the office. You are here to work, and to work hard.

Want to chat with a coworker? You'll need to do it while they are away from their desk getting a quick refill of liquid. Need to take a smoke break? You can do it as long as you get your work done. Most employees are on merit-based pay, where you are paid for what you literally accomplish. So if Jon writes 80 articles in an eight hour day, versus Jeff, who writes 60 articles in the same period, Jon makes more money than Jeff, and they both understand that. Running late to a morning meeting? Do it again and you're likely fired. Openly, audibly yawning in the office? That means you didn't adequately prepare for your day because you didn't get enough sleep last night.

As a recent college graduate, I asked myself, what did I just sign up for!? I came from a work-from-home job that gave me full liberty to indulge in my spoiled, lazy ass habits of bingeing TV shows and playing video games. Now? I start off heading into the office at 7:50 am each morning in the first five months, but after that, I would be "promoted" to join the consultants and arrive at 5:30 am each morning before our mandatory 6 am meeting every day. Then, you could have days where you have eight, hour-long client meetings back-to-back-to-back.

Is this too much for you? Most of you would think so. Some of you may think this environment is inhumane. I certainly thought so at the beginning.

If you want to look up the company, I work for Redmond Growth Consulting. At the time, it was a startup company where my main bosses were a father and son duo, Tim Redmond (father) and Robert Redmond (son). As a helpful reminder, Tim was a guy who grew a software company called Tax and Accounting Software Corporation (TAASC) to a $40 million/year business.

Obsession is Weird

After selling the company to Intuit, and years of traveling ministry work, Tim decided to make a serious charge toward building a business consulting firm. He mentored and coached clients on his own, but now he has his sights set on building a large-scale team again. I joined the dynamic duo of the Redmonds in December 2017, when the firm only had 30 clients to their name. Now? We have quadrupled our client load and we continue to climb to larger goals. The Redmond duo have the current goal of reaching over 300 clients!

To provide tons of back-end services and proven systems to our clients, Tim utilizes a key relationship with an organization called the ThriveTime Show. Clay Clark, the founder of the company, started it with Dr. Robert Zoellner. Combined, these nutty characters have built over 15 multi-million dollar companies, ranging from automobile auctions to DJ entertainment companies to regional banks to marketing agencies.

Understand that I signed up to work at a job where the key partners collectively grew more than 15 multi-million dollar businesses. DJ Connection, Clay Clark's first business, was the largest wedding entertainment company in the United States. Dr. Zoellner's optometry clinic has the highest sales volume per square foot of any optometrist in the country. **Our entire organization, as a whole, proclaims to have helped clients earn more than $2.4 billion in revenue growth.**

This is an environment of excellence.

OBSESSION LEADS TO EXCELLENCE

Pathetically Apathetic

While I have survived and thrived at the consulting firm, MANY people have been fired trying. It's amazing to me that, as an employee of over two years, I'm considered one of the "veterans" at the office. Over the course of two years, I've seen a lot of new, bright-eyed candidates shadow the office and take in all the lights and sounds. There's bumping music everywhere in the office, bells going off when someone closes a lead and lots of enticing activity. At first glance, it looks like a super fun place to work at. But, then, reality hits on the first day.

Everyone starts by either writing search engine content or making sales calls. They are tasked to do one of these things all day, every day. The grind of sitting there and making over 200 phone calls every day gets really old, really quickly. Your first day involves you sitting there with nothing happening and no sales appointments to show for it, because you still suck at the job, AND you likely got cursed at on the phone already. Not really fun anymore, huh?

You look for any excuse to get distracted. You take several bathroom breaks, because you've been "drinking a lot of water." You take coffee trips to get yourself motivated through caffeination. You go outside for a breather, but there's only fresh air for so long. If you don't make 200 cold calls, you'll have a good discussion with the boss on your second day. **Many people have come and gone before the end of their first day.**

I really don't try to explain my work environment anymore. It's just so out of the ordinary. No one would understand why I'm in this job. Why would you choose to get to work at 5:30 am and not leave the office before 6 pm some days? Why would you place yourself under such strict standards? Who would want to work at a place that's this stressful and time-consuming? Turns out...a lot of people.

We run interviews every single week at the office, and there are always people that show up. We'll have weeks where over 50 people apply for a job! Nevertheless, we're only able to find a few good kernels of corn in the sea of...well, crap. Because, out of those 50 people that apply for the job that week, half of them won't RSVP for the interview. Half of the people who do RSVP won't show up, and only a handful will actually dress sharp and act sharp in the interview. Studies reported by *INC. Magazine* show that 85% of people lie on their resumes and 81% of people lie during the job interview. And, even after the interview, it's still not a guarantee that they will make it through our environment!

So, every week, we run interviews and sift through the many unworthy people to find the good nuggets to work with. It makes you think, **why would so many people attempt to work at a place that's known for their stressful rigor?**

I would also ask...why do people want to work at Google? How about Tesla? How about Ernst & Young or Amazon? Why has one company, Paypal, been able to produce six billionaires who are included in what's called the "Paypal Mafia?" Why are the majority of people that work at Life.Church, the largest church in the United States, actually just volunteers? Why does the cast at Saturday Night Live constantly pull all-nighters to come up with jokes that, half of the time, don't land? Why do the athletes for the New England Patriots put up with an almost-dictatorship level of leadership from coach Bill Belicheck?

All of these organizations are excellent. They are at the top of their game, and are not stopping any time soon. They are all obsessed about their trade and relentlessly want to provide excellence in their work. **This obsession is the only reason why these companies are at the top and remain at the top of their industries.**

People see the success and they want it. Who doesn't want to work with the big boys and girls? It's a stamp of approval, a sense of pride to say that you got the "big job" at the top hospital in your city. While working at any of these places requires so much from their team members, these team members gain great lessons, immense fruits and career-altering skills. In most of these cases, they are also well-compensated.

Regularly, people who leave these organizations end up creating their own awesome careers themselves. Certain organizations even specialize in doing just that, like Y Combinator. As one of the best tech startup incubators in the world, they are to blame for assisting with startup tech companies like AirBnB, Stripe, Dropbox, Reddit, Twitch, DoorDash and over 100 other companies, each individually valued at more than $150 million.

Getting accepted into the Y Combinator program is a badge of honor in itself! These hungry entrepreneurs know that getting into the group has created so much fruit for others. Why not for them, too? It's the same reason why people who work at big law firms end up leaving after a few years and confidently start their own firm. They know what success looks like, and they've been able to successfully participate in it. People like to be with the "successful."

There's an issue, though, with all of these "wanna-be ballers." **Very few people are obsessed, and that's why so many fail to hang with the successful crowd.**

No One Likes Obsession

Obsession is Weird

Obsession has a negative stigma tied to it. It's included in many clinical disorders, the most commonly known being obsessive compulsive disorder (OCD). People look in disgust at the straight A student who complains about a 96 on their exam. They see someone who constantly slaves over their work, and they say to themselves, "Man, I do NOT envy her job." They see the guy who's a stickler for the details, and they'll ask him to relax and take a chill pill. They see another woman jogging in the morning as they're dragging themselves out of bed. They think, "Who the hell does this woman think she is? Running outside at 7 am...6 am...5 am...4am??"

Is there a line where it's "too far" in the obsession for success? You know what, I'd say so. You'll find that the leaders of many top companies and organizations are wrapped in controversy. Donald Trump's entire life is wrapped in controversy. Jeff Bezos, Elon Musk, Jack Dorsey, Jack Welch, Mark Zuckerburg, Andrew Carnegie and many of the "greats" all have negative public stories for their careers. These stories include ruined marriages, estranged children, financial fraud, bad experiences from previous employees and many, MANY lawsuits! **Obsession and success does have their consequences.**

For the celebrities who make a living out of their name, they work adamantly to keep their name in a positive light. You can think of people like Lebron James or Kobe Bryant or Ellen DeGeneres or Jimmy Fallon or Kevin Hart. They all, at one time, dealt with negative stories written about them, or some mistake they made, and now, no one even cares. Who doesn't like Kevin Hart?

There's another consequence to being obsessed. **You can't be obsessed about too many things if you want to be truly excellent.** Think about it...do you see Kevin Hart building amazing custom homes? No, he's creating something funny. Humor is his obsession.

Pathetically Apathetic

He's now doing movies, TV shows, clothing lines and other business ventures...but what started it all for Kevin Hart? Comedy! And he'll never ditch comedy.

Lebron James was obsessed with his goal to be one of the greatest there ever was in basketball. It was not until he reached his #1 player status that he began to look at other ventures in business and acting. When he was 23 years old, he didn't know squat about which companies to invest his fortunes in. He was still laser-focused on dominating the sport of basketball.

Another consequence of this laser-focus obsession? You become an unstoppable force, and you do whatever is in your power to keep it that way. That means, **you eliminate any people who will keep you from your end goal.** You know how misery loves company? I can tell you that those who are successful almost express the opposite sentiment. Kevin Hart discussed once, on the *Joe Rogan Experience*, that he needed to cut people out of his circle numerous times. I'd argue that people like Kevin Hart have needed to kick out more friendships and family members than they like to brag about. As Steve Jobs has said about saying "no,"

> *"People think focus means saying yes to the thing you've got to focus on. But that's not what it means at all. **It means saying no to the hundred other good ideas that there are. You have to pick carefully.** I'm actually as proud of the things we haven't done as the things I have done."*

Few people can handle the intensity and obsession all of these stellar people have with their craft. Examine your peers and you'll easily see that most people are not obsessed about anything. All of the people I've previously mentioned had a childlike, and even child-born fixation on their trade. If you listen to enough interviews about these individuals, and read enough books, you'll notice that they all started young. Successful entrepreneurs sold things when they were in elementary school, singers put on performances and shows for their family members as children, musicians began playing their instrument before they were in grade school and the greatest doctors read about science and the human anatomy obsessively in school.

None of these people lackadaisically reached their destination. They didn't wander around from place to place and end up with their glorious lives. **They were all OBSESSED with reaching their end-goal, and they did things very few people were willing to do to become truly excellent.**

What's Left for Us?

We must face reality. The sobering fact about all of these successful names...is that it seems so dramatically impossible to achieve their status of success. Frankly, it probably is impossible. How many 25 year-olds figure out that they want to be the greatest icon in some field and *actually do it?* Very few. You may live the entirety of your life without knowing a single super successful person. I mean, come on, how could I expect to become the next Bill Evans for jazz piano or the next Malcolm Gladwell of book writing at the age of 25 years old? The dreamy expectations that we fantasized about when we were children have now withered completely away, due to our collision with reality.

Let's face it, you probably aren't going to be the "next big thing."

And, since we like to justify all of our life decisions through our self-serving bias, we don't want to say that it's our own faults. We don't want to admit that it could be our own cause that got us to our unsatisfied, current state. **We're masters at the blame game.** Here are a few examples you may have said yourself or heard others say:

- "The economy is terrible. There's no way I'll be able to make a good living."

- "There just aren't any good employees out there. It's not even worth trying to look for them."

- "There just aren't any good jobs out there for my field. It's not even worth trying to look for them."

- "Things have just been really hard and I just can't find the time to care about my fitness."

- "Man, I'd love to read books again. That would be nice…to just have that free time again."

We can think of a thousand reasons why we're not where we want to be. We can easily jump back into "our boxes," as *Leadership and Self-Deception* would say(see page 102), and convince ourselves of anything. We look at the insanity of these obsessed people and say, "Who do they think they are?" We'll do anything to make sure our self-serving bias stays intact.

Because, obsession is weird. It's the kid who loves his guitar so much that he doesn't go out to parties during high school. It's the girl who wasn't the most popular or beautiful, but she's a wizard with video games. It's the athlete who makes no friends on the court, but is the silent killer who drills 3-pointers all day, every day. It's the guy who's so funny that he literally isn't good at anything else. These people are weird, because they aren't like most people. **The sad part is many of us likely had these remarkable quirks and traits, but because being obsessed is weird, these traits were stuffed down, unable to thrive.**

Most people tried many things growing up and never mastered anything. Most people work at a job, make an annual salary that moderately satisfies them and that's it. Most people like to dream about how things could get better, but, when they see the guy who's closing all of the deals every month, they secretly hate him. Most women secretly hate the girl who turned her lackluster physique into the dream body, because again, misery loves company. Most guys beat themselves up with terrible self-talk about how they can't seem to convince any women to go on a first date, let alone other dates. Most people have problems that they can't imagine getting out from under. When most people see that, after five years, someone was able to pay off their student loans, they secretly mutter to themselves, "They probably had someone help them with that. There's no way they did that on their own."

This helps explain why half of all Americans don't have more than $500 saved. That's why 70% of people hate their jobs. That's why you hear people talk about how good it was to be a kid. You think any of these star-studded individuals would want to just be kids again? Maybe so. It's a lot of pressure and attention to be on the top of their game... but they've done a great job at being awesome. Why? They chose to obsessively work toward a goal more than others, and longer than others, until they reached the goal. They destroyed any other ideas of what they wanted to do and dove headfirst into their particular craft.

Are you seeing this now? **Success does not come without obsession.** For many of you reading this book, you never wanted to be a big shot. That dream died a long time ago, or never existed. No matter who you are though, there's something itching at you. You've got some...thing...

Pathetically Apathetic

it's eating at you to finally do it. I don't know what it is, but it could be anything. Reading books, having a better relationship with your kids, actually starting a family, getting better at video games, losing weight, gaining weight, being more friendly, saying "no" more, earning more money, living somewhere else, playing more board games, taking time to explore places... the possibilities are endless!

So, while all of this talk about the obsessions of the very successful doesn't seemingly relate to you, it does matter. Obsession matters, even with the little things. **If you can't get obsessed about never letting yourself drift from your goals (no matter how small they may be), then you will never reach that desired end.**

Or, even worse, you'll just stumble around your goals for much longer than you wanted, never fully accomplishing those goals.

Consider yourself and how you live your life. Is there any part of your life where you are positively obsessing over something? I say "positively," because bingeing a TV show all night or obsessing over how many shots you can do without throwing up isn't positive. That's just my opinion. Is there something you need to freak out about? For example, cleaning your home...do you need to throw your phone in a locked safe for an hour and just go on a cleaning spree? Do you need to cancel plans to keep yourself focused? Do you need to turn off that TV or kick out that pet cat in order to eliminate all distractions? Do you need to freak out at your roommate because they've left those dishes dirty for FAR too long??

What if that roommate gets mad at you and never changes? Do you need to move? That seems a little obsessive...but that's the

point. All of these other bright and esteemed individuals we discussed in this chapter would've done the same things. If they were making sure their home was clean, they would go to no end to ensure they were satisfied. They would schedule consistent times each week that they would never skip. Then they would continually ask themselves how they can improve on their cleaning. They would research online for better products for cleaning, tips for particular stains and "life hacks" to make their lives easier. They would start to get weird, and that's what it takes to get really good.

In order for you to actually get done what you've always wanted to get done, there's no way around it. **Get obsessed. Get weird.** Who cares? Nobody does. Most people are pathetically apathetic, remember?

CHAPTER 6:

Environment & the Mentorship Gap

WHAT MAKES FOOLISH BEHAVIOR BAD?

> *"Show me your friends and I'll show you your future."*

The first time I heard this quote was back in high school during a youth church service. It has a nice ring to it right? It's from the common motivational phrase, originated by Jim Rohn, "*You are the average of the five people you spend the most time with.*" It's, apparently, also rooted in a Bible verse. Proverbs 13:20 directs that we, "*Walk with the wise and become wise, for a companion of fools suffers harm.*"

A companion of fools…it seems odd for me to think that I could be hanging out with "fools." That would be a tough conclusion to come to, especially when you have been with the same friends and family members for years. As you were growing up, these people were always there. The many memories and stories bond people together real tightly. It's oftentimes the "foolish" stories that bond people the closest together!

Environment & the Mentorship Gap

I remember I took a 24-hour road trip from Tulsa, Oklahoma, to Denton, Texas, to see my older brother DJ a gig. He had been a DJ for several years in the Dallas Metroplex, and even got voted as the "Best DJ in Dallas" by Dallas Magazine twice! I had never seen my brother DJ, so I thought it would be fun to drive down there and see him in action. I convinced three other friends to join me for my quick 24-hour trip.

To my surprise, the venue my brother played at was not a dancing venue. It was, really, just a chill bar with a stage in the back. Nobody was in the mood to dance at the venue. You had the typical rustic feel that comes with a burger and bar joint. Out back, there was a spacious outdoor patio with seating, gravel floors, pool tables and dart boards. In the back of all the seating, there was a stage, where a DJ could play music for visitors or a country band to play classic songs. This was not the dance venue I had pictured in my mind. My friends and I were all expecting to do some fun dancing. This night could've been a huge letdown, until we started acting foolish.

Since my buddy and I like to dance, and we were expecting to dance, we basically said, "To hell with it, WE'RE DANCIN'!" So literally, for hours, in front of all these people eating food, it's just the two of us dancing in the middle of this empty floor. Everyone else is just watching us as we dance our butts off. From time to time, people would join in, but they would quickly sit back down and act civilized. We didn't care though. We came down to dance, so that's what we did. It didn't matter what people thought about us, we were just actin' a fool up there.

Pathetically Apathetic

You could consider this an innocent night of fun, but it is kind of foolish behavior, right? Two guys dancing in front of people eating food with no regard for what people think of you? Or, am I just thinking too much about this night in Denton?

We might as well ask, what does acting 'foolish' even mean?

Foolish - "*having or showing a lack of good sense, judgment, or discretion.*"(according to the Merriam-Webster dictionary)

You may not find my story to be a very foolish one, because it's just for one night. Everyone has nights where they disregard the social norms and go a little too far in their behavior. Were we showing a lack of good sense or judgement in Denton? Maybe so. One night where we drank a decent amount and danced a lot doesn't sound bad. But, what do you commonly associate with foolish behavior? Some areas I think of include being a belligerent drunk, getting into fights with people, driving with reckless abandon on the road, acting blatantly disrespectful in an incomedic manner or being loud and obnoxious when you're obviously not reading the room.

The real difference comes when we create close companionships with people who are constantly acting foolish. Guys and girls who are always acting like knuckleheads. People who are running on reckless abandon, who blatantly disobey laws and who never seem to act civilized. People who dramatically react to everything in life. People who will happily "live it up" every weekend, knowing they despise their job or where they live. **The consistency of their reckless behavior indicates that they are committed to "acting a fool."**

It's the friend or relative you know that never seems to figure it out. They are always getting fired from jobs, getting in trouble with people, damaging something and massively forgetting obligations. They always

Environment & the Mentorship Gap

ask people for favors because they're just "in a tight spot." You help them the first time and the second time. But the third or fourth...or seventeenth time? Come on man, get your act together!

Yeah, those are fools.

In chapter 3, we broke down the importance of trusting in yourself and your own capabilities so that we, as a society, can foster stronger trust in each other. In chapter 4, we have our own battles and worlds to improve upon, which is just as noble as saving a nation from starvation. In chapter 5, we saw that those who consistently dig deep and get obsessed about their goals, go above and beyond what they could have imagined. All of these chapters, so far, deal with internal problems. Don't be fooled by the title of this chapter. **Just because we're discussing the quality of our environment, doesn't mean that we can start blaming others for our shortcomings.** Remember the quote, *"Show me your friends and I'll show you your future?"* Which friends, family members and loved ones do you choose to allow in your life?

Let's remind ourselves of the Proverb: *"Walk with the wise and become wise, for a companion of fools suffers harm."* The goal is to become wise, correct? Right now, we're acknowledging some stereotypical definitions of foolish activity. But, let's think a little more "real world" by examining some circumstances that don't seem foolish, but also don't inspire wisdom. How about the couple that never goes out on date nights, because they allowed life's troubles to kill the spark in the relationship? How about the parents that are in constant fights with their kids, but they've given up on trying to seek counsel and guidance, because the last two times they tried, it didn't work? How about the mid-30s guy who drinks by himself, alone, on a weekend, watching sports, instead of honing his skills on woodworking, something he's been wanting to be good at? How about the woman in her early 40s, who's stuck in her human resources field, but she's already thrown in the towel on trying to start her own consulting firm?

If the goal is to become wise, but our lives look stagnant and bland, are we secretly living a foolish lifestyle? Could we be caught up in a world of friends, family members and work colleagues that don't push us to become wise? Could we be in an occupation, a city or a home that doesn't provide the opportunity to accomplish our goals? **Could we be living pathetically apathetic lives, just because we're caught up in the pathetically apathetic world around us?**

We can easily find the foolish lifestyle to be an appealing one. It requires few responsibilities, looks very fun and is ultimately a selfish lifestyle. You could find that the normalcy of your life isn't that foolish. What's wrong with working in a job that just pays the bills? What's wrong with being immensely chill and doing nothing on the weekends? On the surface, this life looks perfectly innocent, but let me remind you about what a good person looks like in my mind: **I believe you're a good person if you live a very intentional life, a life that's dedicated to improving yourself and the world around you.** Design your life influence you to become wise? To be more intentional?

You Can Be Successful and Foolish

It's been profitable for many people to act foolish! It's often the dream for people to get paid to act stupidly. There are many comedians that stake their fame and fortune on acting recklessly. Bert Kreischer is one of the prime examples of making it big out of his tom-foolery. Bert is a stand up comedian that's had a massively successful career

Environment & the Mentorship Gap

touring around the globe. He's friends with other great comedians like Tom Segura, Ari Shaffir and Joe Rogan. He's also starred in his own television shows over the years.

Bert's career got started in 1997, when he was just starting to do stand up gigs. More importantly, though, the *Rolling Stones* magazine put out a story about the biggest party schools and partiers in the country. They named Florida State the biggest party school in the country and guess who they named as the biggest partier in the country? That's right, Bert Kreischer. He's known for performing his stand up sets shirtless, telling stories about inadvertently helping Russian mob members rob a train and constantly getting invited to just party with people. Literally, on one of Joe Rogan's podcasts, Bert describes a gig where he was simply asked to drink and party with white collar business people. That's it.

(Bert Kreischer, The Machine)

It's helped him have massive success, but the entire "foolish" genre of comedy and entertainment makes big money. There's the National Lampoon franchise, with its series of movies, television shows, radio shows and the 28-year long magazine from the '70s to the '90s. There's the show, *Impractical Jokers*, that's been running for eight seasons, since its release in December 2011. The #2 highest grossing comedy film currently is *Hangover Part II*, where the entire premise is based on getting black out drunk and finding out what the hell happened the night before! In some form or fashion, it's the essence of comedy to act like a fool, to do activities that normal people would not dare to do or talk about, for a good laugh. Whether the stories are true or not really doesn't matter.

Bert Kreischer has found it difficult to slow down his party life. For one thing, he's had a great time doing it, with endless stories to share during comedy sets. He's been the epitome of the party life, but now, he's 48 years old, and has a wife and two kids. After decades of partying hard, he's noticing that his average night of eight drinks (for real) is a bit too much. On a visit to his doctor's office, his doctor adamantly said "no more" to his behavior. The doctor basically said "This has to stop or else something will dramatically go wrong with your health." Bert needed to find a way to solve his life issues quickly, so he could just stay alive to watch his kids grow up. **Bert came to grips with the fact that his foolish behavior would ultimately kill him and negatively impact the lives around him for good.**

Thanks to the friends he had around him, Bert actually did find a way out. In the first "Sober October" podcast with Joe Rogan, Ari Shaffir and Tom Segura, the crew decided to rally together in a four-hour podcast to put down a bet. Can we all make it a month being completely sober? No drugs, no alcohol or other substances for an entire month?

Surprisingly, it worked. They all went an entire month completely sober. They've continued to do this two more times since 2017, and many other groups of dudes and dudettes have participated. In fact one of the huge appeals for them to keep going has been the response from fans participating. Rules have changed, and there have been different stakes on the line, but, overall, it's been a positive experience for Bert and his friends.

There's Too Much Foolishness

Don't we all like a good knucklehead, though? They've got wild stories that only ridiculous, foolish people would have. You listen and laugh along as they tell tales of their adventures no sensible person would dare partake in. Part of their thrill in doing the foolish activities is when they explain the elaborate story (which could likely be fictional, but no one really cares when it's a good story). Getting the group to laugh and engage makes this person the life of the party. It brings them attention that they feed off of until the next party. Plus, since they are such a loose cannon, they are totally willing to throw out coarse jabs at people for the wild laughter of the crowd. They are willing to do, and very capable of doing, ridiculous things, while drunk. If someone gives a recommendation to do something stupid, this person will likely jump to action, potentially at their expense.

So, what's the bad part about hanging around with knuckleheads and foolish people again? Don't they just make your life much more interesting and exciting? What would we do without our foolish knucklehead friends? Do not be deceived. While these fun characters live crazy lives, there's a more serious problem with allowing this behavior to be accepted in your own life. **There are too many foolish**

people out there. We've got a mob of them, and only a few people have good, close relationships to turn to in times of turmoil.

What's been revealed about our society, particularly with the rise of social media and the internet, is an alarming amount of people who need guidance in this world. **There are many lost people out there who are searching for SOME positivity.** They have been burned by mentors and close figures in their lives. Their parents were unfaithful and uncaring towards them as a child. They experienced traumatic moments during school with no one to comfort them. For whatever reason, a string of unfortunate events caused a spiral towards a regrettable lifestyle.

So, after living years and years without life going right, a person, let's call this person "Mark," will finally get motivated enough to reach out for help. YES! Mark is seeking a cure for his problems. Good for him! But as we discussed in chapter 4 and 5, **motivation is quite slim.** After several years, and even decades, of floating about in life, how successful can this sudden change in Mark's life be?

When Mark looks for resources and guidance, he first turns to his friends and family. Not surprising that this is a natural first step, right? Most people don't get the best lottery picks in life, though. Mark got stuck in a family that's dysfunctional. He's surrounded by friends who promote foolish behavior. Mark has a long-term, intimate relationship with someone who isn't a positive influence on him. Mark attempts to follow the "guidance" of his friends and family, but, because it's coming from a terrible source, life doesn't get better.

Mark even explores religious beliefs and takes himself to church.

Environment & the Mentorship Gap

While this often does the trick for people, even this can go wrong. Churches aren't perfect, and, oftentimes, are inhabited with people just as dysfunctional as the friends and family members they started with. The only difference is that the church environment has done a great job at covering the filth with smiling faces and the "God-guise," the fictitious feeling that everything's okay if we slap Jesus's name on the situation. In Mark's experience, he attended the church for a couple months or so, but, because he's quite uncomfortable with this environment and no one is going out of their way to welcome him, Mark stops attending the church.

So, Mark tried his friends and family members with no luck. He tried a religion or two, but the people in these religious groups weren't living out their faith lovingly or enthusiastically. This crippled Mark's trust that religion could be the answer. Let's also think about what kind of person Mark is. Mark is like most people. He doesn't have a lot of genuine trust or faith in the goodness of humanity, as discussed in chapter 3. Mark would like to trust people more, but he's had bad experiences, and can't even trust himself to commit to his goals. Mark also wanted to grow up and be a doctor, but finances were tight, and he enjoyed school a little too much, as he got kicked out and settled for a less paying medical job. He was never informed about the harsh lessons of chapter 4 and 5, where, if he wanted to pursue extraordinary goals, he needed to be an extraordinary individual first. And now, Mark feels alone, with seemingly no one in his environment to turn to.

After years of failure, due to poor resources, life becomes pretty demoralizing for Mark. He's come to the grim conclusion that foolish behavior is everywhere, and it's even celebrated by most of the world. **Mark realizes that it's actually going against the grain to seek**

wisdom. It's going against the norm to rebel against rebellious behavior.

There's plenty of people like Mark who at this point, would've simply given up. The challenge is too great to fight and prosper in life, so they choose to settle for what's easily within their reach. But a few people, including Mark, decided to go to a resource that's booming with knowledge...the Internet.

The Rise of Unlimited Knowledge and Wisdom

<u>All hope can't be lost! Why do we see so many people thriving and making a good life for themselves?</u> We see that our environment around us sucks, but obviously, these impactful people we see on television or the news or in articles did something to get where they are at. What did they do?

So, now Mark, like many of us, turns to the Internet. Interacting with the Internet includes its many critical comment sections and forums, but most of us have wised up to the fact that there's a lot of negativity and hatred. There's a lot of blame going around on any topic imaginable. If you aren't careful about who you follow on social media, your page can be rife with this banter. Then you start to believe in the hatred of supreme powers and you become yet another "keyboard warrior." But, as the Internet caught on more and more, good people found ways to promote themselves. Genuinely helpful people saw a platform that can be broadcasted to almost anybody, and they figured out a way to share great insights. What's even better is that it's actually, somewhat working.

Dr. Jordan Peterson is a psychologist who has created a firestorm of popularity. He started back in 2013, uploading his lectures online. He had been a clinical psychologist and professor at universities, like

Environment & the Mentorship Gap

Harvard and Toronto, for decades. As he started to learn about the popularity of Youtube, he wondered if he could be able to engage with an audience outside the classroom. Sure enough, his teachings on "Slaying the Dragon Within Us," and other religious deep-dives, caught on. He saw as many as 50,000 people watch his lectures in the early years. This really impressed him, because, instead of just his couple hundred students in the university, he's now teaching tens of thousands on Youtube.

As his popularity on Youtube was starting to break out, there was a proposed law that included numerous social justice solutions. One of those items included gender pronouns and what people who are "between genders" or non-binary need to be called. The law provided a list of 70+ pronouns that citizens of Canada would be given to use in order to call these non-binary people something appropriate. Citizens in Canada would be required to use these pronouns to acknowledge these people. I won't dive into whether this is a good or bad policy, but Jordan saw eerie signs of Marxism and the Soviet Union in this legislation. He had spent great portions of his life studying these former empires. So, he stood up emphatically against this legislation.

As a result, Dr. Peterson took a lot of flack. At one point, during one of his lectures, he's seen on Youtube being massively booed by a mob of students. Protestors held derogatory posters, called him vile names and cried roaring chants during the lecture. There was no sensibility and no listening, just deafening boo birds. In times like these, it looked ugly for this Canadian professor.

Right when the uproar started against Dr. Peterson's critiques of this legislation, he joined Joe Rogan's podcast for an almost 3-hour interview. In this forum of uninterrupted conversation and endless interview questions from Rogan, the audience in favor of Dr. Peterson erupted. This video, published on Youtube in November 2016, now has over 10 million views. Dr. Peterson spends the interview talking about his escapade against the new policies being proposed in Canada, but also gives many of his, now, classic lessons on the podcast. These included the lesson to clean your room before cleaning the filth of the world. He educated us on the horrors of the Soviet Union and Marxist ideologies. He challenged viewers to take responsibility for life, to start by fixing what's in front of you and to nobly provide relief for those already in their circles.

Here's just a few appreciative comments from his first interview with Joe Rogan:

- *"Jordan Peterson in 2016: 50,000 ppl is crazy reach. I could never sell that many copies of a book. Jordan Peterson in 2019: at least 3.5 millions copies of 12 Rules for Life."*

- *"Just to be clear, my room is clean."*

- *"People say it often, but this podcast literally changed my life. I was in such a dark place, took his advice, cleaned my room and fixed what I could. A year later things got a lot better. After 3, unrecognizable"*

- *"Listening to Dr. Peterson is like having the father I never had. I appreciate everything he says. It's like therapy and guidance."*

- *"If you want to be safe, stay home. Don't come to the university. - (Dr. Jordan Peterson) Aaaaand I'm a Jordan Peterson fan now."*

Environment & the Mentorship Gap

People are hungry for knowledge that isn't provided by their peer groups. Dr. Peterson has been filling theaters with thousands upon thousands of people paying to listen to his lectures in person. That's right. People are paying good money to watch a man give a lecture on psychological principles. Millions of audience members are buying his thick book, *12 Rules for Life,* and legitimately implementing the lessons found in the book. It's shocking to see how an unknown psychologist out in a Canadian university suddenly got bold, stood straight up in confidence (that's his 1st lesson in *12 Rules for Life*) and took his passion into action. **You'd be ignorant to say that Dr. Peterson was apathetic with his life.**

Dr. Peterson isn't the only figure to share wise knowledge online. The rise that we see with these instructional videos and informative interview podcasts online is awesome. You have Master Class lessons from giant, industry-leading individuals that you can receive lessons from. You have websites, like Lynda.com, that've been around for years, giving people online lessons for practical skills. You have many Youtube channels solely dedicated to how the successful mindset works. Some Youtube vloggers, like Ryan Serhant, spend their time creating videos about their lives and the lessons to learn from their lives. You have many podcasts on this topic, as well! It's wonderful and people are finding solutions to their problems by just implementing the strategies.

But, wait a second...I might be too negative here...doesn't it seem just a little worrisome that so few people are actually implementing these good principles? **Do we really need more podcasts, more Youtube channels, more motivational speakers and more books to convey these messages?** I mean, we brought up principles from Dale Carnegie's book, *How to Win Friends and Influence People*, all the way in chapter 3. Don't principles like "smiling more" and "being genuinely interested in others" sound like common sense?

I guess it might sound like common sense to me because I grew up very fortunately. I had both of my parents stay married growing up, and they are still together. That's an anomaly in today's world. Not only that, but they were loving and caring toward me. They continually told me they loved me and they're very happy whenever I visit them. I had successful people around me to give me nuggets of knowledge. Successful business people and ethical mentors in my life lived respectable, good lives. I got to observe how they lived, even if I was still a spoiled, lazy kid.

Not only that, but my family members are all great. We have a network of family members that have, somehow, stayed connected for generations. In 2019, we had a family reunion of 180 people together in Texas! All of these folks had the wherewithal to show up for events during the week, positively participate in the events and interact with each other in a friendly, kind manner. I went to private school all my life and had teachers who actually cared. I had an active lifestyle in sports and could pursue anything that my heart desires.

So, whenever I read lessons given by Dr. Jordan Peterson in *12 Rules for Life* or in Dale Carnegie's *How to Win Friends and Influence People*, it intuitively makes sense. **To those who didn't have the blessings I had? They're just learning these lessons for the first time.** Most people were not given a great deck of cards to begin with. Most people aren't living awesome, thriving lives. That's the problem. The whole environment is in the pits, scraping by! Maybe that's why people feel so inclined to continue to write motivational self-help books. They think the previous ones didn't work.

Environment & the Mentorship Gap

But, this isn't it at all! **The environment we interact with on a daily basis makes a huge difference!** With an uplifting environment, correct resources, watchful guides and helpful mentors, we are constantly affirmed with what needs to take place to improve our lives. Because most of our fathers and mothers didn't listen when these wise counselors gave instruction, the resources didn't make a difference with them. They chose to be apathetic, which causes new generations to continually feel like they need to find the answers.

That's why people like Mark (our fictional character from earlier) will pay big ticket prices to go listen to Dr. Peterson in person. That's why desperate business owners are paying bigger ticket prices to just get the actual answers to success. That's why you find tens of thousands of people listening to folks like Tony Robbins. They go to "find their purpose" and discover what it takes to "motivate themselves to success." That's why people are going to various religious beliefs to discover a deeper meaning in life. **We're all trying so hard to find a good group to do life with.** The resources are available and have been available!

So, why can't we buy into the message? What's keeping most of us from actually seeing the change take place?

It's our environment, people. Again, "*Show me your friends and I'll show you your future.*" Who do you hang out with? Who is dragging you down? Who constantly gets you into trouble? Who makes your life fun for a little bit, but an overall living hell? And, if your environment sucks, then how do you actually improve it for good? In most cases, it takes an extreme environment that's dramatically different from your current world to cause the sudden shift. It takes years of stressful discomfort to enforce the good character traits you always wanted. **It takes a shock to your system.**

Pathetically Apathetic

Great Environments Provide a Painful Shockwave of Positive Change

There's a middle school that started in the South Bronx of New York City called the KIPP School, the Knowledge is Power Program. The school was designed to be the saving grace for minority children in environments of poverty. Only 16% of the kids in the South Bronx education system perform at or above their appropriate grade level in math. In a community where 75% of children live in single-parent homes and 90% of these families need government assistance to chip in for "free or reduced lunches," KIPP is seeking to do the impossible... bring these kids out of poverty.

How has the KIPP School system fared?

Extraordinarily well. The KIPP School system has expanded to 50 locations across the United States. Recruitment is designed via a lottery system, where parents earn the chance to send their kids to KIPP. Why? Because, these children are almost guaranteed to leave their poverty behind. **90% of former KIPP students will receive scholarships to attend private high schools the parents could never afford. Furthermore, more than 80% of these KIPP graduates will go to college.** Before KIPP, few children would find the opportunity to thrive and advance past their upbringing. Now? They have a realistic chance to leave their poverty behind.

What does it take for these kids though? How come the KIPP School is so wildly successful with their teaching? The information about the KIPP school is provided by Malcolm Gladwell's #1 best-selling book, *Outliers*. Let's see what a typical day looks like:

Environment & the Mentorship Gap

1. They begin school at 7:25 am. This is earlier than any average school start time across the United States.
2. From 7:25 am to 7:55 am, they are in a "Thinking Skills" class.
    a. (Was that even a thing at your school?) From here they have...
3. 90 minutes of English
4. 90 minutes of Math (For 5th graders, they spend 2 hours every day in Math.)
5. 60 minutes of Science
6. 60 minutes of Social Science
7. 60 minutes of Music (2x/week)
8. 75 minutes of Orchestra (Yes, this is different from the "Music" class. And, yes, everyone does "Orchestra.")
9. By 5 pm, all classes are over. A majority of American schools end their day at 3 pm. KIPP students spend a total of 9 ½ hours going to classes, eating lunch and having recess. The average student spends a little over 6 ½ hours at school. What else happens in their day?
    a. Children will participate in after-school homework clubs, go to detention and play on sports teams. **KIPP students are often at the school until 7 pm at night.**
10. What's the result of this rigorous school schedule? **KIPP students receive 50% to 60% more time learning than a traditional public school student would.**

Children would willingly put up with this environment?? In many cases, when these prospective children are told about the school, they cry in reaction. I guarantee you there are many kids that start and end up dropping out because of the schedule commitment. Furthermore, a place like this also enforces great standards. They utilize an acronym

Pathetically Apathetic

called SSLANT, which stands for:

- S - Smile
- S - Sit Up
- L - Listen
- A - Ask Questions
- N - Nod When Being Spoken To
- T - Track With Your Eyes

I should also mention that, **they have longer school years than everyone else.** KIPP students go to class on Saturdays from 9 am to 1 pm and in the month of July, there's an extra three weeks of school. From 8 am to 2 pm, they go back and participate in summer school.

But, now that we've seen the schedule of what happens in the school, what does it take for a typical student to actually achieve good results at KIPP?

Outliers, from Malcolm Gladwell, describes the life of Marita, a 12 year-old attending the KIPP School in the South Bronx. Here's what she needs to do every day to thrive at KIPP Schools:

1. The wake up call is at 5:45 am for Martia to "get a head start." (Have you ever heard a kid talk about getting a head start?) The commute requires this for most children in the South Bronx, due to the many bus stops and subway stations. Half the KIPP

Environment & the Mentorship Gap

students actually wake up before 5:30 am.

2. Marita goes to school from 7:25 am to 5 pm and arrives home at 5:30 pm.

3. After that long day at school? She says "hi" to her mom, and then starts homework. If it's not a lot of homework that night, it will take 2 to 3 hours of her time. If there are essays, it could take up to 4 ½ hours. **With breaks for dinner and catching up with her mom, Marita will likely stay up until 11:15 pm!**

4. Sleep and repeat the schedule all over again 6 ½ hours later.

Malcolm describes his amazed response to Marita discussing her schedule with him. *"She spoke in the matter-of-fact way of children who have no way of knowing how unusual their situation is. **She had the hours of a lawyer trying to make partner, or of a medical resident.**"* It's insane to think of these KIPP students doing school like this! Before KIPP, they're used to a much more relaxed, easier lifestyle.

But, let's remember, what are the benefits of a student attending the KIPP School?

1. **Marita gets trained on what it takes to truly work hard.** She knows how to put in the hours to get great grades. She understands what words like "grit" and "self-control" mean.

Pathetically Apathetic

2. The KIPP School is only a middle school. That means there's only a couple years of sacrifice these kids need to make for a lifetime of change.

3. Marita is receiving 50-60% more schooling than her old friends in the public school system.

4. Marita will likely advance to a private school in New York City, instead of falling back to the public school system in the South Bronx.

5. Marita will likely attend college and graduate, because most college students have never illustrated the work ethic Marita implemented during her time in the KIPP school.

6. She'll be like many of these kids in the South Bronx who graduate from college, the first in her family.

Here's Malcolm's conclusion on Marita's life:

"Her community does not give her what she needs. So what does she have to do? Give up her evenings and weekends and friends -- all the

Environment & the Mentorship Gap

elements of her old world -- and replace them with KIPP."

- Malcolm Gladwell

The KIPP School is a miracle to these kids, but it literally forces them into action. It rips them from any means of retreating back to what was comfortable. And, if the children end up not wanting to participate, or, if the parents think it's "too cruel," then they lose their chance. That's the real attitude that wisdom shows to all people eventually.

If you ask and plead for wisdom, you will be granted it with pleasure and abundance. If you continue to ignore the many signals and signs about how life works, wisdom will rebuke you and level you into the ground without mercy. Just read how Proverbs 1 describes how wisdom treats people, and carefully marinate over each verse. It's powerful.

Proverbs 1:20-33: The Cry and Rebuke of Madam Wisdom

> [20] *Out in the open wisdom calls aloud,*
> *she raises her voice in the public square;*
> [21] *on top of the wall[d] she cries out,*
> *at the city gate she makes her speech:*
> [22] *"How long will you who are simple love your simple ways?*
> *How long will mockers delight in mockery*
> *and fools hate knowledge?*
> [23] *Repent at my rebuke!*
> *Then I will pour out my thoughts to you,*
> *I will make known to you my teachings.*
> [24] **But since you refuse to listen when I call**

and no one pays attention when I stretch out my hand,
²⁵ since you disregard all my advice
and do not accept my rebuke,
²⁶ I in turn will laugh when disaster strikes you;
I will mock when calamity overtakes you—

²⁷ when calamity overtakes you like a storm,
when disaster sweeps over you like a whirlwind,
when distress and trouble overwhelm you.
²⁸ Then they will call to me but I will not answer;
they will look for me but will not find me,
²⁹ since they hated knowledge
and did not choose to fear the Lord.
³⁰ Since they would not accept my advice
and spurned my rebuke,
³¹ they will eat the fruit of their ways
and be filled with the fruit of their schemes.

³² For the waywardness of the simple will kill them,
and the complacency of fools will destroy them;
³³ but whoever listens to me will live in safety
and be at ease, without fear of harm."

"You are the average of the five people you spend the most time with."

- JIM ROHN

This will sound cruel, but yes, you should leave your terrible friends. You should abandon family members who are keeping you down. You should move to a new city and stop committing to a dead town. You should keep your commitment with your spouse and figure out how to make it better. If it's an abusive or unfaithful marriage, you should leave the relationship for a healthier life. **Is it harsh to leave your former foolish friends in the dust? I'd argue that you're being harsher against yourself by settling for what's already lackluster.**

Life is harsh. If we can't rely on friends and family to give any comfort or positive guidance, then we must find new ones. We can find a new family that will adopt us into their homes. They are waiting and available if we simply look hard enough. We can find new friends who can give us guidance. Even if we have to sacrifice time and money temporarily to prove our commitment, it's worth it. Even if we need to move somewhere else for a fabulous job opportunity, live below our means for several months, to work our ass off without ceasing, we should do it. It's worth it.

You could have the greatest deck of cards in the world. You could've been the son or daughter to a giant business mogul. You could've been born into royalty in some far off land. You could've been blessed with wealth throughout your life. **This still doesn't negate the fact that, no matter what cards you're dealt, you must play the game well.** That means we need to learn and develop our skills to play the game. How do we develop these skills? **Take the effort to find great people to teach us.**

Change your environment. Change your life.

• • • •

Let's take a quick timeout.

There's some merit to be said for people's uncontrollable circumstances. I did not start life from the pits of hell. I had a great advantage. I mean, come on, I'm a white dude in the United States who got his college paid for. The fact that I'm writing a book on "apathy" could be insulting for some of you.

I need to take a pause here and say something important. **Nothing is insurmountable.** Just trust me on this. This isn't just some motivational phrase people throw around. If you dig deep enough into the many "started from the bottom, now we're here" stories, you will find people are capable of amazing feats. While I blame my life transformation on a higher power (my faith in Jesus Christ), tons of men and women around the world have simply decided something important for their lives. **They decided to take ownership and no longer be a victim.**

Nothing I have written (or will continue to write) is revolutionary. There's no "secret" or "one trick to turn your life around." For the rest of this book, we will dive into the practical steps that you can implement TODAY to create positive traction on your life. I will continue to describe real examples of how this works. In my life or in other lives, it still works the same. No matter how long it takes, it still works.

Your environment may be terrible. You may not currently care about anything. You may not have any obsessive drive at all. Your goals and obstacles could look monstrous to you. You may have been screwed a hundred times and trust no one. **Nothing is insurmountable.**

Now, back to our feature presentation.

Environment & the Mentorship Gap

CHAPTER 7:

Apathetic vs. Non-Apathetic:
A Case Study

I'm very new to the diligent doer, non-apathetic lifestyle. It's great that I've been able to make steps towards taking care of responsibilities, identifying goals and being more intentional with my life, but I'm still new at this. It's only been three years that I've spent living a disciplined life and planning out my time. **Three years is not a long time**.

Just for full transparency and clarity, here are the spots that I can still improve in (among other areas):

- **I don't want to serve people**. I'll take out the trash at my office here and there and offer to buy things for people, but there isn't consistent service. **I have yet to, as Jesus Christ talks about, become an obvious example of servanthood.** As it's said in Mark's gospel in the Bible, "*Whoever wants to be a leader among you must be your servant, and whoever wants to be first among you must be the slave of everyone else. For even the Son of Man came not to be served but to serve others and to give his life as a ransom for many.* (Mark 10:43-45)"

Apathetic vs. Non-Apathetic: A Case Study

- **I'm not a very obsessed or passionate person.** Sure, do I need to be a passionate person out of necessity? Of course, but that's the only reason. I'm not the guy to get fired up about a cause or some trivial calamity happening in people's lives.

- **I don't always honor my personal responsibilities.** It's a hard skill to master for most, and I've certainly gotten better, but I'm not there yet. As Matthew 5:37 says, *"But let your 'Yes' be 'Yes,' and your 'No,' 'No.'"* When I put something on the calendar for my job, I'll get it done because that's how I get paid. When I schedule something for myself? Ehhh... not so much.

- **I'm not as genuinely interested in people as I'd like to be.** It's one of the core principles from Dale Carnegie's *How to Win Friends and Influence People*, but I fail to find myself caring about other people. Friends and colleagues will ask about how my day or weekend went, yet I struggle to remember to ask them the same questions.

There are many shining examples to look at from this book! Dr. Jordan Peterson has become a saint to many men in North America. In Canada and the United States, this man has become the father figure they never had. He's dealt with immense backlash, hatred and disapproval for simply laying out the facts of life. He becomes a target, because his honesty stings, but that's exactly what our men and women need! A good prick in your side brings pain and that's one of the world's greatest motivators.

Pathetically Apathetic

Justin Wren is a man who's built a non-profit organization out of sheer willpower and overwhelming compassion. He's corralled a great team of people to work with him and, as a result, he's built 100 wells in Africa. That's phenomenal! Each well brings fresh water to thousands of people, which saves their lives from very easily treatable diseases. But, remember, this was after years upon years of living recklessly. He spent years in drug use, alcoholism and the glamour of fame. He needed to go to hell and back to become an inspirational figure.

Great teachers from the past and the present came from various unfortunate places. Dale Carnegie pursued a failing acting career before becoming a public speaker and best-selling author. After Dale performed a road show, he arrived back to New York in his mid-20s with no job, broke and living in a local YMCA.

Andrew Carnegie (no relation to Dale), was a Scottish immigrant who would start working at the age of 13 in jobs that required 10 to 12 hours per day of work, for 6 days each week. His family was not wealthy at all, with his father struggling to keep employment. As we read already, this didn't stop Andrew from becoming one of the wealthiest and charitable individuals the world has ever known.

Kevin Hart was declared by TIME magazine in 2015, as one of the 100 most influential people in the world. You wouldn't have believed it in his early years, though, when his father was a cocaine addict who was in and out of jail and Kevin lived in a single-parent home. Jim Stovall became an Olympic weightlifting champion, best-selling author, television network creator and multi-millionaire, all AFTER turning blind in his mid-20s. Sean Stephenson spent 30 years of his life doing motivational speaking in front of millions of people, became a best-selling author and defied countless odds. The countless odds originated from osteogenesis imperfecta (a disease that causes your bones to be extremely brittle). He recently passed in August of 2019, yet he wasn't even supposed to survive his birth.

I can imagine some of you reading right now could look around and find some great leaders and mentors in your world. They aren't super prolific, successful people, but they've built a good life. Maybe there's just one aspect about a person you know where you say, "Wow, I'd love to be like that, someday."

In a single week, I identified three instances where three people in my life were very conversational and genuinely interested in people. Because of their genuine interest in others, one of these people was well-known by gas station employees and graciously greeted with kind conversation. Another one of these people left a restaurant with coupons for a free meal because he genuinely made the manager's day. The final person couldn't help, but have people come by and say "hi" in the middle of our conversation together. I see how well-received all of these individuals are and I think, "Man, they must really care about these people! Everybody loves them! Why don't I?"

Three years is not long enough. A transformation from being an apathetic, lazy person takes YEARS of time to foster and develop. But, where does this all lead to? Where are we headed when we decide to be a passionate, caring individual?

What does it look like to reverse a lifetime of unplanned apathy? We've discussed plenty of statistics, figures, famous examples and stories, but let's do a side-by-side comparison. I read two books that provide this great comparison. The two books tell stories about two people's lives. One book, *Apathy and Other Small Victories*, talks about Shane's life. The other book, *The Happiness Project*, talks about

Gretchen's life. If we look at both of their stories, what can we learn?

Shane's Life from *Apathy and Other Small Victories*

Shane is a man who's pathetically apathetic. He may be the very definition of this phrase. He's been drifting around from city to city for a while now, becoming more and more comfortable with the Greyhound bus system. He's not an arsen, a convict or a serious criminal of any kind. **He's just a man who has thoroughly and completely settled for no more than what's easily available to him**.

In this book, he gets into quite a pickle. He's become tangled in a murder case where a friendly aquaintance of his, Marlene, gets killed. The police have come over to his place and asked him various questions about his whereabouts on the night of the murder. He's not giving a very good impression to the police, though, because he sleeps in a barren apartment with a mattress filled with salt shakers. It's never explained why he steals salt shakers, but when cops find you hungover out of your mind, on a mattress filled with salt and you're a suspect for murder? Not great odds for Shane.

He's also just recently been fired from a temp job at an insurance company. The woman he's been sleeping with, Gwen, introduced him to the job and gave him a recommendation to work there. But, for the next several months, Shane has spent his days at the office sleeping on the toilet, drunk out of his mind and internally criticizing any aspect of the corporate world. I'll let Shane describe to you his daily routine at the office.

Apathetic vs. Non-Apathetic: A Case Study

"I'd stumble into the office and go straight to the bathroom and pass out. When I woke up an hour or two later I'd still be ragged drunk or in the early stages of a debilitating hangover with permanent nerve damage to both my legs. Getting back to my chair was a Greek tragedy of chemical imbalance and full-blown cerebral palsy. I'd stagger past co-workers and fall into cubicle walls and I didn't ever care that I was obviously hammered and reeking of stale cigarettes and alcohol and that there were swarms of fruit flies nesting in my hair.

Delightful guy, right? He ended up getting fired because a long-time employee in the office died and he decided to not go to her funeral. When he selfishly ignored the requests of both his boss and lady friend to attend the funeral, he was dismissed from the office. You should also know that the landlord of Shane's apartment building is tied into the murder case and Shane's been sleeping with his wife.

The book is filled with crude, hilarious dialogue and scenarios, but it can't be refuted that Shane is a pathetically apathetic man. After everything in his life comes to a stressful standstill, and Shane is waiting to hear a decision from the police on the case, he gets vulnerable about his apathetic humanity. He's considering what it would take to change his ways. Here's some of Shane's inner dialogue:

Pathetically Apathetic

> *"I was hoping some terminal illness euphoria would kick in, and that since I knew I had a death sentence hanging over me I'd immediately learn to cherish each day and every breath as a beautiful, wondrous gift from the God I now desperately believed in, and that I'd vow not to waste any more of my precious life that would very soon be ending. Then I would go out and hug strangers and sing out loud and twirl around on top of a mountain like the fucking Sound of Music and be inspirational and brave. Maybe then I could finally do all the things I'd been putting off all these years.*
>
> *Unfortunately I didn't know what any of those things were.* ***It takes more than one kick in the pants to reverse a lifetime of unplanned apathy.****—It takes a special, ironic kind of person to use their own impending death as an impetus to finally live."*

I see this book as more than just a comedy, but actually a tragedy. Shane is a man that finds his own apathy troubling, but fails to make any efforts whatsoever to fix his life. He recognizes that his life's problems could be solved quite simply with proactive action, but he doesn't care enough to take any proactive action.

For instance, he clearly hates his job at his insurance company, Panopticon Insurance. If you couldn't tell from how he spends his days at work every day, then you might need to read about his daily routine again. Sleeping on toilets all day to the point of nerve damage in his legs, then stumbling drunk with numb legs to his desk, without bothering to shower or take care of his own health? He clearly does not want to be there. Yet, even with these clear facts, he struggles to simply quit and move on from this job he loathes. Here's Shane describing this dilemma:

Apathetic vs. Non-Apathetic: A Case Study

> *"I just couldn't take working at Panopticon Insurance anymore.* ***Changes had to be made, but I didn't want to be the one to have to make them.*** *I figured if I was drunk all the time I'd be even more obviously incompetent and they'd have no choice but to fire me. As bad as it was I couldn't bring myself to quit.* ***Quitting is too proactive,*** *and it reflects poorly on a person's character. Nobody likes a quitter.* ***I would always rather be a victim of circumstance."***

When a man would rather be a victim to his circumstances than proactively fix his situation, you know that he's pathetically apathetic. And sadly, so many of us can relate! Because, remember, "*It takes more than one kick in the pants to reverse a lifetime of unplanned apathy.*" As I've already referenced, Shane has many life revelations toward the end of the story, when he's being investigated by the police and there haven't been clear answers for Marlene's death. Here's Shane discussing his regrettable experiences in this new city:

> *"There comes a time in every man's life when he wakes up drunk on the toilet and begins to doubt the choices he has made. And when that time comes at least twice a day, every day, something needs to be done. But what? And how?* ***These are hard, entirely unspecific questions. And apathy has its own slow momentum. It doesn't like to be disturbed."***

No, it doesn't like to be disturbed. I'm sure you (the reader), have noticed this by now. Once apathy has a stranglehold of comfort on our life, it's quite difficult to rip it from its grasp. What Shane ultimately accepted about his life is that you do, in fact, need to rip the apathy. You need to murder apathy. You need to pulverize it and pile drive apathetic behaviors into the ground. Completely decimate it.

For most people, that's too ugly of a proposition, so we go for the half-baked, easy solutions that don't work.

That's what Shane concluded. **He's content enough with the ridiculousness of his mediocre life to continue living as the victim of what life throws at him.** And, you know what, good for Shane. It's odd to applaud an apathetic man, but at least he has accepted that he'll never change. It's a melancholy applause, but it's better than not addressing your trust issues and believing you still want to change. **I'd rather you accept that your life will never get better, than continue lying to yourself that you'll eventually figure it out.**

Gretchen's Life from *The Happiness Project*

Gretchen is the exact opposite of apathy. She's a woman who's interested, passionate and enthusiastic about her life. Even better than that, she is a REAL PERSON! How Gretchen spent an entire year of her life inspired millions of readers to address issues in their own lives. While Shane may be the most extreme example of a pathetically apathetic human being, Gretchen is a great example of the proactive, passionate human being we need to be.

Gretchen Rubin asked a question that everyone has likely asked themselves, "*What do I want from life, anyway?*" It's a funny question coming from Gretchen, because she's already been quite accomplished at this point in life. She graduated with an undergraduate degree and law degree from Yale and became editor-in-chief for the Yale Law Journal. She clerked for a judge in the U.S. Court of Appeals and with Justice Sandra Day O'Connor in the U.S. Supreme Court.

She then turned to working as a lecturer with the Yale Law School

Apathetic vs. Non-Apathetic: A Case Study

and Management School, in addition to serving as a chief advisor for the Federal Communications Commission. She's also married to a great guy, who works in the finance world, and has two kids, living and thriving in New York City. Simply put, she's already doing a lot of good things.

What Gretchen dealt with was something different. As she puts it, ***"I wasn't depressed and I wasn't having a midlife crisis, but I was suffering from midlife malaise—a recurrent sense of discontent and almost a feeling of disbelief. Can this be me?"*** It's often a recurring thought for anyone who's naturally a go-getter, which Gretchen undoubtedly is. This first book, *The Happiness Project*, was a *New York Times* Best-Seller and two of the next three books she would release also received the same acclaim. She's not joking around with her life! And, yet, she oddly seems to face a sense of discontentment. As she puts it:

So, in the high-achieving, Gretchen kind-of-way, she decides to dedicate an entire year to making her life happier. She would embark on what she calls a "Happiness Project." Every month of the year, she would dedicate it to a certain theme of activities and behavioral changes. She started the month of January with "Boosting Her Energy" by doing activities like going to sleep earlier, organizing the home more efficiently and exercising better. Then in April, it would shift to "Lightening Up" by singing in the morning and acknowledging the reality of people's feelings. Then in August, she would focus on "Contemplating the Heavens" by reading *Memoirs of Catastrophe* and keeping a gratitude notebook.

What's great about how she writes this book is that **she doesn't ignore the odd nature of this challenge.** How much better can life really become by doing this? When she proposed the idea to friends and family members, she was met with animosity and skepticism. Here's how her own husband was the first to question the validity of this project:

> *"I don't really get it," Jamie said as he lay on the floor to do his daily back and knee exercises. "You're already pretty happy aren't you? If you were really unhappy, this would make more sense, but you're not." He paused. "You're not unhappy, are you?"*

Gretchen appeases her husband by responding that yes, she is happy. She explains as well that, apparently, 84% of Americans ranked themselves as 'very happy' or 'pretty happy.' Again, Jamie asked her a completely valid question, *"So if you're happy, why do a happiness project?"* Since she's just proposing the idea, she has a difficult time explaining why she needs to do it. Here's her attempt:

> *"I am happy—but I'm not as happy as I should be. I have such a good life, I want to appreciate it more—and live up to it better. I complain too much, I get annoyed more than I should. I should be more grateful. I think if I felt happier, I'd behave better."*

She's never done anything like this, nor has, really, anyone else. How can she know how successful this will be? She's also similarly confronted by one of her longtime acquaintances with this response:

> *"You're not a regular person. You're highly educated, you're a full-time writer, you live on the Upper East Side [New York City], your husband has a good job. What do you have to say to someone in the Midwest?"*

Apathetic vs. Non-Apathetic: A Case Study

This is often a trap many skeptical people fall into. If your life doesn't exactly fit my situation, how can it apply to me? This thinking is so narrow-minded. So, you're saying that because someone wasn't poor out of their mind, didn't have an abusive background or wasn't wasting away part of their life, their story doesn't matter? It's not inspirational? **Well good, have fun trying to find someone who fits your exact expectations.**

In fact, I find Gretchen's ambition quite inspiring (and so do the millions of readers that purchase her books or read her blog). When someone who's up at the top of the earnings pyramid says that they want their life to be happier, this should elevate us normal people to a higher expectation. Gretchen's critics propose that she should be thrilled to have the life she has! And, she is happy, but **she just wants to see if there's any possibility that she can improve even more.** That's a huge character trait of someone who's passionately caring about their life.

So, how does the experiment go? She finds a few activities that really bring more positive results to her life. The first major victory was how she discovered her love for order in the home (i.e. no clutter). She begins discussing this section by divulging research that states, "*eliminating clutter would cut down the amount of housework in the average home by 40 percent.*" She not only found this to be the case for her, but she also loved to effectively remove clutter from the home. From the master bedroom, to the kitchen, to the living space, and even the closets. It was as if she was a kid in a candy store. Here's her talking about some of her revelations with cleaning the clutter:

> *"An empty shelf meant possibility; space to expand; a luxurious waste of something useful for the sheer elegance of it. I had to have one. I went home, went straight to my hall closet, and emptied a shelf. It wasn't a big shelf, but it was empty. Thrilling."*

Have you ever imagined cleaning a shelf as thrilling? I sure haven't. For Gretchen, though, as early as the first month, she found a positive, happy habit for her to utilize for the rest of her life. Way to go, Gretchen!

She did find some plans not going as smoothly as she liked. She would realize, over the course of the project, that **you can't bully people into being happier**. People will do what they do and they will improve themselves as much as they'd like to. We can be helpful and provide plenty of examples, but, if we overwhelm people with too much of what they don't want (even if it's good for them), then they'll just resent us. The closest example she faced, as she describes here, was with her husband.

> *"He drives me crazy by refusing to carry various husbandly assignments, then surprises me by upgrading my computer without my asking. He makes the bed, but never uses the clothes hamper. He's bad at buying presents for birthdays, but he brings home lovely gifts unexpectedly.*
>
> *I had come to understand one critical fact about my happiness project.* ***I couldn't change anyone else.*** *As tempting as it was to try, I couldn't lighten the atmosphere of our marriage by bullying Jamie into changing his ways.* ***I could work only on myself.***"

Apathetic vs. Non-Apathetic: A Case Study

A critical fact indeed about self-development: it's about yourself. Getting emotionally-invested into other people's improvements is a dangerous game. People are unreliable, especially when they're trying to change the way they've been living their life. Haven't we all been pretty unreliable whenever we're motivated to improve, for instance, our cooking skills?

Gretchen also realized during this year of happiness that **she needs gold stars**. Well, she thinks she shouldn't need them, but she knows that words of affirmation, one of the five love languages, is a key point of satisfaction and happiness. The problem is, as Gretchen just explained, we can't bully people into appreciating us. As Gretchen was improving the apartment space more and more, she wanted great words of affection for her efforts. What did she receive?

> *"I was thrilled with the improved conditions in our apartment, and I kept waiting for Jamie to say, 'Boy, everything looks terrific! You've done so much work, it's so much nicer!' But he never did."*

This is a continuous struggle throughout Gretchen's book. **Gretchen likes her gold stars, but few of us liberally dish them out to people**. Don't you find people are hesitant to compliment each other? We all like to be appreciated, but since so few are open about complimenting people, so few feel appreciated for their efforts, just like Gretchen.

So, is Gretchen truly happier after all of this effort? After the entire year of effort, activities and resolutions, she found the whole project to be a success. You could be a skeptic and say that she said it was successful because she doesn't want to spend a whole year doing something and say it was a waste. That's not very motivating! She finishes the book by challenging us with this statement:

Pathetically Apathetic

"Sometimes I succeed, sometimes I fail, but every day is a clean slate and a fresh opportunity. I never expect to be done with my resolutions, so I don't get discouraged when they stay challenging. Which they do."

THE POLAR DIFFERENCES BETWEEN SHANE AND GRETCHEN

(1) **Anything that you continuously need to do is considered worthless by an apathetic person**. This is the first stark difference between Shane and Gretchen. Shane would never have Gretchen's attitude about life, because it's not worth his time. He sees no benefit in marginally improving himself, because it's marginal. And, since the dramatic change that Gretchen has implemented takes decades of time, the Shanes of the world would say, "Ahhh who gives a rat's ass anyways!? It probably won't happen to me."

(2) **An apathetic person's mind is always about the short-term.** What can I receive from life right now? Shane operates on a very impulsive, reactive approach to satisfying himself. How can I have sex even if it's not the best sex? How can I still get paid while working as little as possible? How can I escape something I don't want to do as quickly as possible?

Gretchen operates on a higher level and asks better questions. What activities can I do now to make my life happier now AND in the long-term? How can I make sure to enjoy everything great in my life as much as possible? How can I truly savor what's glorious about today and elongate this feeling for as long as possible? **Gretchen is tapping into a level of life satisfaction that the Shane's of this world will never get close to reaching.**

Apathetic vs. Non-Apathetic: A Case Study

(3) Pathetically apathetic people always choose the easiest way out. It's so easy for Shane. While it's not glamorous, and while he's always poor, he can leave any trivial situation with a snap of a finger by taking a Greyhound to the next city. He can dodge controversial issues by not getting involved. He will always fail to develop long-term success, but he'll succeed at eliminating as many responsibilities as possible from life.

Gretchen, to her own fault on some occasions, will never rest or be content. If she just settles for her current life, she'll continue in her "midlife-malaise," as she calls it. She wouldn't discover how to control her anger. She would never realize that she just loves kid's books and doesn't like jazz. She would never know how invigorating an activity cleaning clutter was for her!

(4) Pathetically apathetic people will always be victims of the world. Shane will never take the world by force or claim his destiny. He's never going to stand up for anything. He'll never be an influential figure, even in his small world, because as he said himself, *"I would always rather be a victim of circumstance."*

Gretchen will always be a victor in her world. She will continue to be a successful individual in her world, because she won't let herself become a victim. She's too busy writing best-selling books, invoking positivity in the world, serving as an advisor and working as a great mom to spend time pointing the finger and blaming the world. It takes so much time and adds so much stress to your day to complain and whine about how bad life is. Just take action and make life as good as you can. That's what Gretchen did, she took action.

Victims accept a mindset that says, "I can't do anything about this and there's no point in trying to fix it. Why can't someone fix it for me??" The trouble with a statement like this is there are truly hopeless victims in the world. There are kids in adoption centers who may never have real parents. There are girls who are abducted every day and are sentenced to a life in the sex trade. There are men and women who were separated from their spouses and will always be haunted by their loneliness. There are people at home and in far-off countries that have no idea how their lives could improve. Real victims are out there.

Here's a tough question to consider, though: **is it better to accept the unfortunate circumstance or die trying to make things better?** I'll let you deal with this question on your own, but for most of us reading this book, we honestly aren't paralyzed by the world around us. We're really just paralyzed by our apathy. We're paralyzed by our inaction. Even if the road ahead is difficult and requires years of sacrifice, we can still massively improve ourselves.

The real question you'll need to answer is this: **are you going to settle for being a Shane or sometimes fail and sometimes succeed at being a Gretchen?** You really aren't at risk of dying while trying to make your life better, so what's stopping you? If you do decide to be a Shane in the world, then great, I applaud you. You have come to terms with reality, while most are still fooling themselves. If you decide to be a Gretchen, I applaud you even more.

Just know that becoming a Gretchen isn't the easiest road. I'm happy to talk to you about what it takes in the chapters ahead, but you must know that you chose the difficult route. You chose to take the red pill from *The Matrix*, instead of the blue pill. Come on, let's find out how to get this done.

Apathetic vs. Non-Apathetic: A Case Study

CHAPTER 8:

Most Will Not Follow Your Lead

Congratulations! After reading so many pages of this book and persevering despite all odds, you are committed to no longer being apathetic. I'm proud of you! Since you're so excited, you'll want to take action. After you see the results taking place, you'll want to tell all of your friends and family how they can take action, too!

You will become a leader. Whether you like it or not, this is a fact of living the non-apathetic life. **Living any lifestyle that's against the norm of the world will cause you to be a leader.** As you consistently take action and see the positive change taking place over a span of years, people will begin to ask questions. They'll get interested in how you live your life and what you do. Since you are now a changed person who lives a passionate lifestyle, you are totally game for helping people!

For instance, you make time at 4 pm one day for someone in your schedule and you head over to the coffee shop to visit them. You're just excited to be able to work with someone on the same lessons you've learned! It's 4:05 pm though, and they haven't shown up. They send text messages or calls to let you know if anything happened either...I guess just wait? They finally arrive 15 minutes late. That's fine, I guess... so you carry on. You explain your pathway to a positive life and share the many lessons you've learned. You instruct them on the specific steps they need to take. But, then, they ask the many "what if" questions.

Most Will Not Follow Your Lead

The person you arranged coffee with confronts you on the many issues overwhelming her. After hearing how you persevered and got intentional, she says, "Oh that will never work for me...or, you don't know how crazy my life is...or, I have this and this and this going on right now...or, that sounds really difficult, I just don't know about it..." You attempt to help explain how simply it can work with anyone's life, but they keep beating down every solution with a different excuse. After over an hour of this back and forth conversation, you feel like no progress has been made. You may even feel like you've been a failure at communicating the idea.

Do not beat yourself up. The sad truth is that few people will join you. You will have many who try, but many more will settle for an easier, lackluster style of living. They see the pains and struggles you went through for years upon years and they're intimidated. They can't come to grips with the reality that tremendous change happens over a long stretch of time. So, they walk away from your positive coffee conversation without any real intention to implement what they learned from you.

Clay Clark, the founder of the Thrivetime Show, and one of the partners of my consulting job, realized this same thing. He had sold DJConnection.com and just started helping business owners who asked. As a result, his methods worked and those businesses grew. So many people asked him for his assistance that his wife actually gave him the feedback that, "Hey honey, maybe you should get paid for dramatically improving people's lives?"

So, he started a marketing and consulting firm that's gone on to be wildly successful. Clients grow, on average, 62% year-over-year, and many business owners see even crazier numbers. Shaw Homes, Oklahoma's largest homebuilder, was a $30 million business before

Clay, and in three years, reached over $80 million in total, revenues. Tip Top K9 was a dog training company that existed for nine years, stuck at the same revenue level. There were only two people in the company (the founders) and they wanted to make this business work for THEM, not work them to death. So after four years with Clay, they have turned Tip Top K9 into a thriving dog training school in Tulsa, Oklahoma (the headquarter location), and they have sold several franchise locations across the United States.

Here's the grim truth again. **For the thousand positive testimonials from clients who saw success, there are four thousand business owners who found the success insulting.** They saw what it took and didn't want to buy it. It didn't matter how many testimonials and best practice examples you gave these business owners. They still wanted success to be a snap of a finger. Here's what you should know, reader:

> WHEN YOU REACH A VERY SUCCESSFUL PLACE IN LIFE, YOU WILL NOTICE PUSHBACK FROM THOSE YOU TRY TO HELP.

And, no, this doesn't just mean monetary success. Remember, I consider you a good person if you live a very intentional life, a life that's dedicated to improving yourself and the world around you. Most people aren't living intentionally, and intentionality annoys them. **When misery loves company, and you aren't part of their company, the miserable crowd resents you**.

Our consulting firm still helps out plenty of business owners, don't get me wrong. I have a catalogue of clients who I personally worked with for years and they saw tremendous growth. We've had business owners across the country thank us for the great work we do. We teach them the real truths about growing a business and provide them the tools to get their business growing. It requires dedicated, hard work, but after just a few months of dedication, it becomes so much easier for the once struggling business owner to now thrive. There's a reason why Redmond Growth has grown from 30 clients to 130 clients in three years. This stuff works! It even worked for my sister who wanted help with managing her life.

My sister doesn't own a business, but we talked during Thanksgiving about how I've positively grown in my life and what our consulting firm teaches business owners on time management. She then replies, "I feel like I have no command over my time or schedule! Can you help me??"

I enjoy this relationship a lot because, (1) she's not paying me so I feel no pressure to "keep her as a client." (2) If she starts to become uncoachable or distracted on our calls, I can simply say this isn't a good fit and stop doing these weekly sessions. (3) She's doing her action items! I feel no pressure to "make her grow faster" to validate paying me, so we can go as slow as we need. She's already seeing benefit in just a month of weekly calls and action items. **Someone who is coachable and is willing to do the action items will always see great results.** That's a fact!

Pathetically Apathetic

(My Sister with her three kids)

The problem arises when someone looks for help, but they are not responsive to the methods. It's annoying when someone needs the tools you've mastered, but they question the validity of doing anything you ask them to do. It's frustrating when your friend is asking you for advice, but they want you to do everything for them. In really, few are willing to ask themselves the tough, honest questions about what they're willing to do. As one of the great leaders of America put it,

"Rarely do we find men who willingly engage in hard, solid thinking. There is an almost universal quest for easy answers and half-baked solutions."

- MARTIN LUTHER KING JR.

So Will We Change?

The depressing answer is that most won't...but why shouldn't you? There've been plenty of facts and statistics and studies about the realities of humanity here. You've read about people who are making a tremendous impact. You've read about my life and how I'm making steady improvements to be less apathetic.

So, why shouldn't you be able to change? Take a look at what's going on with your life and ask yourself, "**What's a real, simple thing I could do right now?**" Pick one thing in your mind to focus on. Here are a few examples of what this mental thought process should look like:

1. *"**I want to lose weight**. Well, to start with, let me sign up for a gym membership and I guess I'll commit to going to the gym...three times per week? I think that's doable. Maybe. In fact, I'll schedule a time today to go to the gym. When should I work out later this week?"*

2. *"**I want to actually have financial savings**. I don't want to be in constant fear that I'll be out of money. Okay well... what if I saved...3% of my income? So, if I make $2400 per month, that's $72? No, that's too much. Let's just save $50 this month. I can eat five meals at home instead of going out this month, right?"*

3. ***I want to make more friends**. Not just more friends, but better friends. Well, I gotta start somewhere! Isn't there that Meetup.com website? I'll check that out and attend a hangout. Maybe I could ask my coworkers if anything fun is happening? Wait...I don't like my coworkers...except for Dave. Dave is a pretty good guy. Let me go see what he's up to. Wait...there is that one guy I knew in college that's in town this weekend. What the heck is he doing!?"*

Do you see how these are just first steps? Sign up at a gym. Save $50. See what Dave is doing. In these next few chapters, I'll go into the lessons that were taught to me by my consulting firm on what it takes to live a non-apathetic life. But the first issue to solve actually has nothing to do with specific action steps or tools. What it takes is a heart that's willing to change, which is oftentimes the first obstacle you'll have to overcome.

Most Will Not Follow Your Lead

CHAPTER 9:

But, Wait...Do You Really?

"You must be cautious, because making your life better means adopting a lot of responsibility, and that takes more effort and care than living stupidly in pain and remaining arrogant, deceitful and resentful."

- Dr. Jordan Peterson

Reading a book like this should give you inspiration to change. I mean, heck, you made it this far in the book. You're obviously liking it for some reason. This book has likely caused you to think about what you could do to improve your life or show more care. "Hmmm... self, what areas of my life am I apathetic about?" Even if it's just to reconnect with an old friend, you feel invigorated. If you are like me, you've already come up with some pretty intriguing ideas about what you should do as a result of this book.

Want to see what taking action looks like? We did this in the beginning of the book, but you've got a new vision on life after these last few chapters. You're now committed, so here are examples of some action steps you'll find a committed person would do.

But, Wait...Do You Really?

Examples of Taking Action

Let's say you don't like how abortion rights are threatened in your state. For that matter, it's threatened around the world. You had a personal story about a friend who got an unplanned pregnancy or maybe you had a really close call yourself. Because of this personal story, you are motivated to make sure more people can have access to affordable, safe abortions. What can you do? A few things as a matter of fact!

First step is to look into Planned Parenthood's website and read about their "Take Action" or "Volunteer" pages. Their first suggestion is to call and email your senator about your feedback and opinions on Planned Parenthood. You can also call and email your state representative about your views. While you do this, I'd also go on Facebook and search for abortion rights groups in your local city. If your city is big enough, there will likely be a Facebook group for abortion rights.

To get smarter about it, you should first reach out to the representatives or senators who are in favor of abortion. If you live in Iowa, for instance, you could get in touch with Senator Claire Celsi, who's been a democratic senator featured in recent articles about legislation on abortion. She's a new senator who won her seat in 2018, so she'll likely use her fresh motivation to help anyone. Senator Celsi isn't the only ally either! Since abortion is pretty much a Democrat vs. Republican topic, the easiest way to figure out who your allies are is by simply Googling "democratic Iowa senators," and picking a Wikipedia page with a list of elected members.

Once you've reached out to all of them several times (don't stop until you get a response), a few will respond back about your inquiry to help out. By building these connections in the House and Senate, you help these elected officials understand that there are people who still want rights for abortion. On top of that, these elected officials will already have ties to local organizations and events that you can participate in. They will point you in the right direction once they know that you truly care to get involved and help out. That's why I emphasize that you call and email frequently, until you get a response. You may even need to SHOW UP in person to get a response! **Do what you've got to do!**

If you want to try and reach out to Republican members to sway them on a specific abortion bill, it would be unwise to attack them on their views. Elected members in the government are VERY loyal to their party. Since Republicans are just about unanimously anti-abortion, you will gain no progress trying to immediately convert them.

What you do is angle the conversation toward how a specific piece of legislation could directly impact you negatively. If you have a heartfelt conversation with a Republican about how restricting this one piece of legislation will be, about how it will result in a real, terrible circumstance to happen in your life, it might create doubt in their mind...and empathy.

Legislation isn't the easiest thing to read, so work with your new democratic allies to decipher weak spots. The best weak spots are ones that have nothing to do with the "moral implications of abortion." In order to sway a Republican towards delaying an abortion ban, or even killing it, find weak spots in spending, implementation and/or the language of the bill. If there aren't too many weak spots to exploit, have your democratic ally add amendments to the bill that morph it into a piece of legislation that Republicans don't actually want. All this being said, these are long-term moves, and your real best bet is to simply remove the current Republican members of the Senate and House of Representatives.

But, Wait...Do You Really?

While you wait for the next election to come by, donations always help out! It seems like a simple, uninvolved gesture, but it's especially helpful if you are busy, but still want to commit some effort to the cause. You can donate directly to Planned Parenthood, or put your donations toward paying for someone to do the relationship building with elected officials on your behalf. You know, fund someone's efforts to reach out to congress and stoke the fire. You could also chip-in financially for someone to go through with their actual abortion.

If you don't have any finances to spare, you can volunteer your time. The best thing for a cause (aside from money) is crowd participation. You can participate in planned events advocating abortion, volunteer to help out at your local Planned Parenthood health center or simply bring encouragement for people who are currently in a tough spot because of restrictions on abortion. You can post about abortion articles and topics regularly on social media. Not so much that you lose friends, but, maybe once per week, you could post an informative story or article about abortion.

Now, if you've spent years trying to sway your government to look more favorably on abortion rights, and you've made little traction, you might consider moving to a different city or state. There are just some states that are deeply Republican and will not budge on their views. Unless you'd like to spend as much as a decade to gradually change the mindsets of the people in your state, you should likely move somewhere more liberal and abortion-friendly. The states of Oregon, California, Maryland and Vermont are currently viewed as the best states for women's reproductive rights.

• • • •

Pathetically Apathetic

This is all a starting point towards pursuing and advocating this specific cause. By starting here and diligently taking action, you turn yourself from a normal, apathetic human into a caring, empathetic person. Sounds great, right!? Well, at least for me, advocating abortion rights, participating in rallies, and calling senators until my head explodes? That doesn't sound so great. Sorry, not sorry. But remember...

That's okay.

You can't care about everything. I know I've spent a good majority of this book preaching about how most people barely care about anything, but this lesson applies to folks who are slaving away with too many things. While most people do not care, there are people on the other side of the spectrum that care about every single little thing. They are the social media commentators, who write up a storm on any controversial topic. They are the people that care to share their opinion about everything. They are the people who say "yes" to everything and, therefore, have no time for anything they actually care about. In fact, these caring individuals help so much with other people's problems and agendas, they have no idea what they actually want or care about. They are the people who get emotionally caught up in the smallest of details, and always feel passionately about fixing every problem. These are the super empathetic people in our world. While we appreciate the immense empathy they give, it's many times, too much to bear for one person.

Please understand that there are only 168 hours per week. **You can only put your care and attention into so many things.** What you'll find is, if you say "yes" to so many things, everything becomes mediocre. You make no progress on the concerns you're *genuinely* concerned about. So, if abortion is something you say you care about, then you should put action into helping out. This is true, even if it's as little as donating a certain amount of money per month. If you can't provide the finances or the time to genuinely help out, then don't beat yourself up. If you genuinely wanted to help, you would make the time to help.

• • • •

But hey, abortion could've been a little too controversial to start with. Instead of choosing a big issue that alters the moral compass of our society, you decide to choose something more light-hearted and enjoyable. You want to learn a new language. There are income benefits to fluency in multiple languages, particularly in southern states where you are given thousands of dollars in additional income every year. You may want to travel, and not look like an idiot tourist. Maybe you married into a family that speaks another language, and you feel really weird when they begin speaking Italian to each other. You just want to learn another language!

Does this goal to learn a language help change lives and improve the world's ecosystem? Not likely (unless you're a translator in a terrorist hostage negotiation). Again, this book isn't about you turning into a roaring advocate for huge causes and abandoning your current surroundings. **The whole point is just caring more about your life and intentionally living to improve and grow.** The whole point is to stop being apathetic! Learning Italian to speak to your in-laws is a really admirable pursuit! Think of the bond you will now have with that entire side of your family as a result!

Where do you begin?

First step, you should probably take a class. Your city may have local classes you can pay to join and get started learning Italian. If you need a classroom setting to learn better, then this will be your best bet. If there isn't one currently, who's to say you can't start your own? What if you connected with a member of your wife's family, inspired them with the idea, spread the word on social media or local poster boards and coordinated a class of a few people every week? You now have a local Italian language class!

There are also very effective online resources, like Rosetta Stone and Duolingo. Both have thousands of testimonials on their successes with people learning languages. Duolingo did an experiment on their own to see if their language application really did the trick. It turns out that 34 hours of practicing a language on Duolingo equates to a semester-long college course. **If you just planned to work on learning a language for two hours every week, you'd get through a semester of development in less than five months!** If you're just getting started, research shows it's a quick transition from novice to advanced language skills. In research conducted by Roumen Vesselinov, a research associate at the University of Maryland in Baltimore, he commented to Vice magazine that the jump from novice to advanced is "*noteworthy*."

The downside here is going from pretty good to fluent in Italian. This is where Vesselinov's research shows a lack of progress. With an app like Duolingo, it's much harder to improve once you've mastered the basics. This isn't necessarily Duolingo's fault. You'll commonly find that with any skill, it takes longer to reach an expert level versus a pretty good level.

If you really want to get to that next level with Italian, your best bet is to simply start talking more and more to fluent Italians…in real life. So if you are married into that Italian family, time to give real conversations a try. It will be rough and awkward, but very much worth it. Once they see that you have worked at this, they will definitely try

But, Wait...Do You Really?

to help you out. For a fully immersive experience, you can travel to Italy for a period and just live. No English allowed! You must survive and thrive by speaking Italian! College classes are actually structured this way when studying languages. You can also participate in real conversations through online chat rooms. There are plenty of apps and websites like HelloTalk or Tandem Language or Facebook/Instagram Messengers that will connect you to tons of people around the world.

Can a 23-year old Learn Jazz Piano?

Learning Italian and advocating for abortion rights are two completely different activities to get passionate about. Both can be just as valuable. Why? **Both inspire you to move toward accomplishing a positive desire**. If you learn Italian, then you now have the ability to build greater connections with more people. Plus, you are more interesting than most people just by learning a 2nd language. I hear Italian's a pretty romantic language too, so your spouse should appreciate it (hubba hubba).

If you work on advancing abortion rights, you connect with people who are as passionate as you are, plus it gives you something to work on. You invest your time into something bigger and bolder than yourself! With both activities, you are no longer living an apathetic life.

I began to enjoy singing at 14 years old through jazz music. I was staying up late one night watching random movies. On the television came Mel Gibson's critically-unacclaimed film, *What Women Want*. In the movie, there's a scene where he's deep into some wine and listening to this guy named Frank Sinatra. The song that played was "I Won't Dance." I thought it was such an interesting voice, much different than any other music I'd heard so far. After the movie, I spent hours digging

Pathetically Apathetic

into his music and got obsessed with this prolific hollywood music icon I had just now discovered. From there, I wanted to learn to sing like Frank.

I got better and better, but it became more obvious that singing like Frank Sintra wouldn't grant me much of a career. I'm quite certain Michael Bublé will be the last great crooner. Even with my singing dreams likely killed, I still listen to jazz music to this day. I'll listen to three or four-piece sets from the Vince Guaraldi Trio or Bill Evans or Miles Davis or some of the many other artists on my "Jazzy" Spotify playlist. Since I always listened to this music while studying or reading books, my desire to play piano like these guys continued to grow. Finally, around my 23rd birthday, after years with this nagging interest, I convinced myself that I was tired of not knowing how to play the piano. I drew up a powerful scenario for myself. I asked, "Alright, self... if I'm on my deathbed decades down the road from now, and I don't know how to play piano really well, will I be disappointed in myself?"

(A Group of Jazz Musicians)

But, Wait...Do You Really?

Setting up a dramatic scene for your future really helps determine whether you truly care about something or not. It forces you to see how important this activity or plan really is to you. My scenario was, "If I'm on my deathbed decades down the road from now, will I be disappointed if I don't take action?" It's harsh, but those are usually the best scenarios to create. **If you're willing to die trying, then you're undoubtedly committed to the goal!** In this case, I said "yes." I told myself I would be disappointed with how I lived my life if I didn't get good enough to play jazz piano like these musicians, the musicians I listened to all the time!

Once I realized this, I contacted a few music instructors, started taking weekly piano lessons with one, committed to 3 hours of practice per week and never stopped. Did I have weeks where I barely made progress? Oh, yeah. I've totally blown a few weeks. On the other hand, there were some weeks where I practiced for 5 or 6 hours.

After taking action with my first piano lesson, I couldn't lie to myself and say that just starting was good enough. A lot of people just start things. Remember how 8% of all New Year's resolutions actually get accomplished? **Starting something is exciting. It's so exciting that most are willing to throw away the long-term satisfaction of excellence to continually ride an emotional roller coaster**. It's a theme ride that soars high during honeymoon phases and catapults flat on its face during quitting times. Like an addictive drug, the dreadful lows are only alleviated by tapping back into the original high of the drug.

Time and consistency illustrate the seriousness of our intentions. As a result of just a couple years of consistency, I've gotten good enough to record my own music and even teach beginner piano lessons! Amazing! And, just think, because I've proven myself to be consistent with piano, imagine how much easier it will be to translate this to everything else in life? My relationships with friends and loved ones...my successful employment at Redmond Growth...my workout regimen...my aspirations to become a ghostwriter, all seem a little nicer to handle now. As Luke 16:10 says from the Bible, *"One who is faithful in a very little is also faithful in much, and one who is dishonest in a very little is also dishonest in much."*

Do You Really Want This? Think Long and Hard.

Why was I able to actually keep this actually going, in particular? In the past, I envisioned tons of "passions" or "goals" that never turned into anything significant. What was the difference between my passion for learning piano versus my passion for...tennis? I remember really wanting to get great at tennis growing up, to play professionally on the Wimbledon courts. I watched guys like Roger Federer, Rafael Nadal and so many others excel. I would actually try to imitate their movements in the living room as they played back the replays. I would play in competitions and actually won some matches. I would track how tennis players were doing competitively. I was INTO IT...or so I thought. My tennis career stopped short once my improvements became harder and harder. What's the difference between my desire to get good at tennis and getting good at piano?

I actually wanted to do it. I wanted to make calls to piano teachers. I wanted to buy equipment for lessons. I wanted to commit to scheduling three hours of practice per week. I didn't need anyone else's financial support or approval for my decision. No matter what was going on, I never stopped. I had fostered a passion for this music by listening to it for years. Through previous choir classes, on-stage singing in musicals, recording sessions in my bedroom and casual listening while studying, the desire kept nagging at me. **After all of this pent-up desire, I just HAD to take action.**

Look for this sensation whenever you're considering what to pursue. **If it's to the point where you just HAVE to do it, you're probably ready.**

On top of that, I didn't fall for the mistake I made with tennis. With tennis, I always had these giant visions of myself playing at Wimbledon and creating a money-making career out of the sport. But, without the intense obsession (chapter 5), the realistic expectation-setting (chapter 4) or the motivating environment to work my ass off (chapter 6), this couldn't be possible. I didn't have people cheering me on to be a phenomenal tennis player! I didn't eat, sleep and play tennis every single day, like the actual professionals would've done. I was unknowingly setting myself up to fail and be disappointed.

For jazz piano, I knew from the beginning that there would never be a chance that I could become a big name in the jazz music genre. My goals were realistic, and I was happy with them. I understood that this goal of mastery with jazz piano wouldn't happen in less than five years. That's why I committed to 3 hours per week instead of 10 hours per week. I knew from the beginning that, if I just kept at it for 3 hours per week, I would get better and better and better.

It's so simple, yet, everyday citizens of Earth decide to do new things all the time. After a day…a week…a month…a year later, we stop doing it. We lose our pace, maybe try a couple times to recover, to no avail, and then, eventually quit altogether. Then we justify this decision to quit. We say things like, "You know, this isn't really for me…maybe this just isn't my season to do this…maybe I just don't have it in me…

Pathetically Apathetic

maybe God's not calling me to be great at this..."

How about this...**maybe, we really didn't want it that bad.**

During Jim Stovall's public speaking engagements, he talks about this "one-size-fits-all" excuse to life. For anything we want to do in life, there is just one excuse that is actually plausible. While we can psych ourselves into believing there are no excuses, he actually gives us one excuse we can use to get us out of anything. Here's what he would say at a public speaking engagement:

(Quote posters in my apartment)

But, Wait...Do You Really?

"Here's the one size fits all excuse for all situations where any area of existence isn't going the way you want it to go; look directly into the mirror at yourself and simply say,

'I guess I really didn't want it that bad.' - No other excuse matters."

I have this quote hanging on my wall (see page 181) with many other posters of quotes and influential figures. I want to frequently remind myself that it's really as simple as saying, "I didn't really want to do it." It pisses me off, but at the same time, it's brutally true. If a guy who turned blind at the age of 25 was able to become an Olympic weightlifting champion, write a hugely successful book, turn it into a major motion picture and create an impactful life for himself, what's to say that we can't? Who gets in the way of our ability to build a life we actually like living?

Oh yeah, ourselves... because we're pathetically apathetic.

There's no secret to this, readers. Everyone we've read about in this book bought into the same narrative. Whatever cause or life change they wanted to make, they wanted it enough to make it happen. Their empathy and compassion was so undeniable that they couldn't live with themselves anymore. They had to take some kind of action. They had to quit associating with the wrong friends. They had to stop their addictions. They had to travel to that foreign land and work with these people for the rest of their lives. They were willing to die in order to reach their goal. All of them pursued their goals with this burning passion that wouldn't stop until the goal has been achieved.

Like I've said before, this book was written in an attempt to erase the cognitive dissonance we experience in our lives. And, no, I don't care that I'm beating a dead horse here. I want to beat this point into your skull until you finally get it!

You should not feel deeply hopeless about your current "lack of compassion" to change the world or yourself. Everyone lives this way! This was written to inform you that, instead of sleeping in and completely blowing off your weekends, you can find activities that give you more meaning in life. You can work towards earning a certain income or find a loving partner for life or live more adventurously. You know what, you could actually be very passionate about hibernating on the weekends and designing a life where you can sleep all weekend. Who cares?? No matter what this goal is…

IT WON'T HAPPEN IF WE CONTINUE TO TELL OURSELVES THAT WE CARE…WHEN WE DON'T. TRUE CARING OCCURS WHEN ACTION TAKES PLACE.

In regards to what you do, that's up to you, and you alone. As for me and my priorities, do I have the ability to go serve my time at a homeless shelter and pass out food to people? Definitely. Do I have money to contribute donations to kids in 3rd world countries so they can eat adequate meals? Yes I do. Could I reach out to my old friend and rekindle the relationship with him, have phone calls with him and even take road trips down to his place for visits? Yeah, I could make time for that. I could do anything under the sun, but I choose not to do those things.

Maybe I'm not the saint Mother Teresa would want me to be right now, but you know what I am? I'm pretty happy with what's happening in my life. At the time of my writing this passage, November 2019,

But, Wait...Do You Really?

I work at a job where I save or donate 30% of my total income and live well within my means. My coworkers like me and they are very enjoyable to work with. I'm actually planning to give them all a Christmas gift, all 47 of them in the office. I live in a nice apartment in downtown Tulsa, with a view down the Arkansas River. I get to practice piano, workout regularly, read books frequently, hang out with friends and still get to watch great TV shows. As a result of all these things, I've been given the opportunity to pursue genuine passions, like writing this book! I'm able to pay for piano lessons every month and I give myself time each week to practice. I repeatedly invest time to think about my life, which helped me figure out that piano and writing were two core activities I wanted to excel at.

I didn't have any of these things after college. Back in the summer of 2017, I had just gotten out of college, without a job. I spent more than a month sleeping on couches until I found some job. That job was a stay-at-home job where I cold-called people to participate in paid research studies. It sucked my soul and I grew depressed, because I existed by myself every single day, every week. I barely hung out with friends and, whenever we got the chance, they were convinced I was getting depressed! I had no enjoyable hobbies, no consistency and little vision for my future. **All I had were great dreams, goals, hopes and expectations for my life, but no way of seeing how I could fulfill these expectations.**

• • • •

It's obvious that you want to be able to diligently pursue some passion or interest. You wouldn't still be reading this book if you didn't (thank you for still reading, by the way - you are a great gift to humanity). You would love to be able to start a new hobby, take action on a certain cause you think is horrible, improve your life in a positive way and/

or break off some bad habits. Before we go down the blazing trail of fulfillment and passion, **it's essential for you to figure out whether you really want it that bad.**

- If you'd *kinda like to* help drill water wells internationally...

- If you'd *kinda want to* start a business...

- If you'd *kinda wish* you could learn a new language...

- Even if you deeply desire to learn how to snow ski, but *the timing isn't right*, **you don't want it that badly.**

Justin Wren (all the way from chapter 1) lived in the Congo for a year, used car wash soap every day, slept on the dirt grounds and got malaria multiple times, to the point where he almost died. Walt Disney went bankrupt with his business ideas three times before building his future empire, Walt Disney World. Jim Stovall lost his eyesight in the prime of his life and went on to build a television network...AS A BLIND MAN. These people obviously wanted it.

Is it unfair for me to compare you to these great titans? I don't think so at all, and, in fact, because you think it's unfair, that tells me you don't want it that badly. I'll let Napoleon Hill explain very simply,

> *"The only limitation is that which one sets up in one's own mind."*

(Napoleon Hill wrote one of the greatest self-help books in the past century, during one of the most trying times around the world - The Great Depression.)

But, Wait...Do You Really?

If you do want it, that's fantastic, and I applaud you for your bold compassion towards this goal of yours. **What's not okay is waking up every morning and telling yourself how "uncompassionate" you are compared to that friend who shipped himself out to Asia and now lives with native people in huts.** If I choose to practice piano for three hours per week, that means I can't live with native Vietnamese people in huts. During those three hours every week, I can't hang out with friends, sleep more, play video games or help out at a homeless shelter, because I'm playing the piano. I don't feel ashamed or weird about it, because that's what I want to do. This is what's important to my life.

Determining Your Goals - Your F6 Goals

In order to be less apathetic about our lives and other people, **we first need to know what we actually care about right now. More than just words, what are you willing to do right now?** This process of figuring out what you like and don't like could take hours and even days to break down. It could take years to finally come to grips with. No matter what, this question must be answered.

No matter what the answer happens to be, the answer is okay. Newsflash, you may not want to change at all! If everything is really going the way you want it to right now, and you're completely satisfied with life, then screw me. Close this book and feed it to your dog. But, if you want to grow, advance, develop and create a better life, then **you have to know what you actually care about.** One of the best quotes on this topic comes from Jack Welch, the former CEO of General Electric. In his 20-year tenure at General Electric, between 1981 and 2001, he grew the company's value by 4,000%. He says, with immense clarity,

Pathetically Apathetic

"Face reality as it is, not as it was or as you wish it to be."
- Jack Welch

Let's start with simply jotting down all the interests, passions and goals you *think* you have. I want to stress this, **the first time around, you are wrong about the goals you actually want.**

I remember a period of time where I was fairly convinced that I would be willing to invest years of scheduling to become a CPA. One semester of online classes made it very clear that this was NOT my passion! **Do not feel immense pressure to determine your ultimate future right now.** Just jot down ideas and, after implementing steps to address these interests, you'll figure out which ones you're willing to put the effort into. You'll find out what you honestly care about.

Thanks to the consulting firm I work at, they give business owners a great way to break down goals that are important to their lives. This is what my bosses call, the "F6 Goals." Each of the six "F" categories represent a central area in your life. **Write down what goals/desires/interests you have for the next year in each category**. Please, don't feel like you have to create your five year or ten year plan for each category. If a year is too far away, what do you want to accomplish in the next three months? Or just the next month? Maybe just this week! Here are some questions to ask yourself in order to help stir up some ideas:

- » What's not happening right now that I want to happen?
- » What small actions could I take in order to improve this area?
- » What good habits have I been putting off?

But, Wait...Do You Really?

- » What do I wish I could learn or do, but just haven't gotten the chance to do?
- » What's an easy thing I could do right now?

Finances:
_____
_____
_____

Fitness:
_____
_____
_____

Friendships:
_____
_____
_____

Family:
_____
_____
_____

Faith:
_____
_____
_____

Fun:

_____

_____

_____

I've attached below the first time filling out my F6 goals back in Spring 2018. I had a friend of mine help me determine these. This is a great idea during this exercise. **Have a trusted friend with you** to bounce ideas off of and simply ask you questions like, "Okay, how will you do this?" or "Why do you really care about that?"

Harley's F6 Goals (Spring 2018)

Finances:

- Invest 5% of my income into a mutual fund
- Save 15% of my income (10% -> Roth IRA & 5% -> Savings Account)
    a. Total Savings? = 20%
- Earn $50,000/year at my job

Fitness:

- Work 3x/week at a minimum, barring illness

[I only wrote down one fitness goal. I was not confident in this category at all. In fact, this continues to be one of the areas I struggle to maintain the most. You may find that after years of trying to implement these F6 goals, you still find difficulty getting it done.

But, Wait...Do You Really?

Remember, **if you really care about it, you'll work your entire life to get it accomplished.**]

Friendships:

- Find 5 consistent friends in the Tulsa area
- Have reliable buddies to hang out with for the fun activities I want to do

Family:

- Talk to my parents every week
- Get to know all of the family members in their 20's and build a relationship with them.

Faith:

- Find a Young Adult group to join
- Find a service, local outreach to participate in
- Listen to sermons in the morning prior to work

Fun:

- Identify consistent hobbies and activities I want to participate in:

    1. Golf
    2. Tennis
    3. Ski Trips
    4. The Arts
    5. Reading
    6. Piano
    7. Writing

- Identify consistent activities I'll do on a weekly basis:
  1. <u>Golfing</u>
  2. <u>Panera Bread</u>
  3. <u>Reading @ Coffee Shops</u>
  4. <u>Fun Planning (to organize things with friends)</u>

It makes me laugh to see these old goals I had written down. **I can't stress enough that the first time you do this, it won't be pretty and perfect.** For FUN goals, I put down "The Arts" as a consistent activity. What the hell does "The Arts" mean? There are also no ideas written downon how to actually accomplish these goals! **Be specific!** Then for FAMILY goals, meeting all my relatives who are in their 20s was an idea. That quickly got removed because, after digging into it, I found out that there weren't many other cousins or family members in their 20s like me. On top of that, I just didn't care about that.

Is it okay to say that I don't care about knowing distant cousins and relatives in my same age group? YES, THAT'S OKAY. **The only way to validate your interests is by proving it through action.** After you've jotted down your F6 goals for the next year, **write down all of the various interests and passions you have for your entire life.** Here are some more questions to help give you ideas:

- » What are those things you want to change or get involved in?
- » What causes do you want to influence?
- » What are you wanting to get compassionate about?
- » When I die decades down the road, what will I regret not doing or learning?

But, Wait...Do You Really?

_____

_____

_____

_____

_____

This could be a monumental moment for you. Do you realize this? **There are many people out there that have never written down their goals.** They've never put to paper what they actually want to do. There's immense power in writing it down, because now the dream is taken out of your head. It used to be imaginary, and now, it's one step closer to reality.

Honestly, deciding to play piano was crazy impactful for me. It's such a simple thing. It's so fulfilling to actually do something you have been wanting to do for several years. Now, I'm actually good at it and I now have this burning fire to get better and better and better. People in the office know me for my piano skills now. If I never took the step and committed to it, it would've never happened.

One more thing before we move on, **please don't immediately post on social media or the internet that you are committing to accomplish these new goals of yours.** I get it. You want to broadcast to the world how awesome you are. You're proud of yourself! You're using social media to help pressure you into actually doing your goals. Here's some honest feedback...no one cares. And, for the few people that would care, just talk to them directly about it. You also don't want to be that guy or gal that posted about the goal and then failed to do it. **Give yourself a couple months prior to sharing anything about this.** We now have our big list of ideas. Let's keep going.

Pathetically Apathetic

CHAPTER 10:

"Be Fruitful, Then Multiply."

My boss, Tim Redmond, often uses this quote for our work. As you already know, we work with business owners to help them gain financial and time freedom. The work could range from helping a plumber find more workers to hire, to accurately tracking revenues and expenses to truly see how profitable the company is. Business owners, unsurprisingly, get excited about growth. When the first boost of business occurs, they get about expanding or even paying off huge portions of debt. Signing a lease on new office space, quickly hiring new team members, and diversifying with different services are typically next steps. Too often, though, these moves are premature.

What my boss will say is, "Be fruitful, then multiply." The point is that you don't want to simply equate a successful business to more and more sales. If you only rely on more sales every month, slower months will inevitably come and cripple your business. If you simply rely on word-of-mouth business (people bragging about your company to friends and family), the sales will eventually fizzle out, since you aren't consistently advertising your work. During that slow time, you lay off half of the great team members you worked so hard to acquire, and you now have no need for the sweet office you signed a lease for.

Before you go crazy about growing your business, our consultation dives into building the systems necessary to scale out your business.

"Be Fruitful, Then Multiply."

We put together tracking spreadsheets, so you know the status of leads coming into the business. We schedule meetings each week for staff training and strategic planning, so you are proactively moving one step ahead. How do you expect your staff to improve more and more each week if you aren't dedicating time specifically to make them better? We have our clients use a tight calendar and to-do list to make the most of their day. More importantly, we need to consistently be profitable. Our business owners aren't receiving millions of dollars of funding to create the next big tech startup, so we concentrate on what they need to do each week to sustain healthy profitability as they grow.

Be fruitful, then multiply. This works the same way with your life.

Did you magically become the kick ass person you are today? No, of course not! You had to grow up and mature. You had to learn some harsh lessons and get rejected by people. You needed to learn what it's like to live in the real world, rather than the fairytale world you saw in kids' movies. Before you were able to run, you had to be fruitful with walking. Before you made your first group presentation, you had to learn how to communicate properly, as a child. Before you drove a long road trip across state lines, you had to get in an empty parking lot and have someone teach you. **You were first fruitful in the smaller things so that you could be tasked to deal with bigger things.**

We need to stop setting ourselves up for failure here. Too many people want to go move a mountain, when they first need to clean up their messy home. Dr. Jordan Peterson discusses this in his book, *12 Rules for Life*. Rule #6 states that we should *"set our house in perfect order before we criticize the world."* If we don't know where to start "being fruitful," let's look at some suggestions that Dr. Peterson gives us:

Pathetically Apathetic

"Consider your circumstances. Start small. Have you taken full advantage of the opportunities offered to you? Are you working hard on your career, or even your job, or are you letting bitterness and resentment hold you back and drag you down? Have you made peace with your brother? Are you treating your spouse and your children with dignity and respect? Do you have habits that are destroying your health and well-being? Are you truly shouldering your responsibilities? Have you said what you need to say to your friends and family members? Are there things that you could do, that you know you could do, that would make things around you better?

Have you cleaned up your life?"

In just one paragraph, you have a whole year's worth of action. And, while there is a lot to tackle in this paragraph of deep questions, he asks you to first consider your circumstances and start small. **You may simply need to enhance what you already have.** Start small by doing what you realistically can do. If you know you can't consistently do something on a daily basis, then why not weekly? Instead of starting something new, maybe you become more consistent with something current. Finding this out will only come through trial and error. In the first round of F6 goals, I found out which things I didn't care about, the things I did care about and the slight pivots to more successfully execute my plans. **This is not a one-time activity. This is your life.** In fact, after creating your first F6 goals here in the book, go through your F6 goals again two months from now.

There's a Bible verse that backs up Dr. Peterson's 6th rule in Matthew 7:5 that states, "*You hypocrite, first take the plank out of your own eye, and then you will see clearly to remove the speck from your brother's eye.*" **Multiplying fruitfulness implies that what's already there is fruitful.**

"Be Fruitful, Then Multiply."

In what you're currently doing, are you really the best that you can be? For example, in the current job you work at, are you the best person there, or are you dispensable?

But wait, what if you don't care about being the best at your job? What if this job is temporary because it makes you money?

Sounds like your goal should be finding a new job! That sounds like an amazing goal! Be like the minority of workers out there who ACTUALLY LIKE where they work. But, before you throw a desk and storm out of your workplace, consider this...**if you are doing a poor job at your current place of work, why would the next job, your dream job, want to hire you?** If it really is an awesome company you're trying to work for, they'll want to know where you previously worked at. What do they need to know about your relationship with them? If it's sour, that doesn't shine a positive light on you. It creates doubt. Even if it's a completely terrible job you are in, and everyone there is annoying to work with, be careful to not operate "within the box." Remember our brief lesson from the book *Leadership & Self-Deception*? Communicating to the future employer that your current job is shitty because of that bad boss and those annoying-ass coworkers and how unbearable your days are? Now you sound unbearable.

Imagine, after six months of waiting to go to the employer of your dreams, you finally sit in on an interview. When they ask you about your previous employer, you'll be able to justify your value with clear indicators, like showing up on time, all the time. You're dependable on the job and work efficiently. You go above and beyond by addressing issues that aren't in your jurisdiction. You compliment coworkers, in order to make the environment more pleasant. You provide such good service that it surprises customers, and they remark about your work. **That's valuable. It's particularly valuable when it's a consistent trait**

Pathetically Apathetic

in your workday, not just "when you feel like it." Furthermore, it's even more valuable when your dream employer finds out about the truly shitty circumstances you dealt with WHILE being an A+ employee.

Take the lesson from Dr. Peterson. Clean up your life. Take the lesson from Tim Redmond. Be fruitful, THEN multiply.

• • • •

But, wait, what does it look like to "be fruitful, then multiply?"

Let's say you want to lose 20 pounds, before the summer comes, for the "summer bod" goals. An admirable endeavor. You currently don't go to the gym and your eating habits aren't the best. Where do you start? Well, I think we all know where the painful beginnings lie. You need to go to the gym regularly. The more frequently you venture to the gym, the faster the results, in most cases. At a minimum, you should go three times per week. It's better to go more times, but let's start with three trips. Then, along with that, we need to eat healthier, correct? Well, what do you eat on a regular basis?

The first step that personal trainers often do is have you journal what you eat in a given week. But, since you are a bright individual, you already know some foods you should remove or include into your diet. Foods like cake, candy and desserts can be cut out. Going to fast food restaurants does not help, either. Start with one item to eliminate and one item to add. For example, you could cut cookies out of your diet and replace it with carrots. If that's too much, just take out the cookies from your regular consumption or add the carrots into your regular consumption.

"Be Fruitful, Then Multiply."

After you have done this for one week, add to the load. Run at a faster pace while at the gym three times per week. Eliminate one more thing from your diet. Add new foods to the diet that need to be consumed. Decrease the amount of calories you eat each week. Pick one thing at a time and always improve on those first goals! Don't be the girl who can get to the gym three times per week, but says, "Okay cool! I hit my minimum requirements. I'm sure I'll hit my goal someday." **Someday is a very dangerous word for your future.** In fact, here's what Tim Ferriss has to say about the word, "someday."

> *"**Someday** is a disease that will take your dreams to the grave with you. If it's important to you and you want to do it "eventually," just do it and correct course along the way."*
> Tim Ferriss
> (One of Fast Company's "Most Innovative Business People" and one of *Fortune Magazine's* "40 Under 40.")

The word "someday" is a curse word in my book. Someday may never come. That's why, whenever you've proven yourself to uphold your beginning goals, you can improve upon them. If you falter, go back to the prior step of the process and prove yourself, again. For example, if you've been going to the gym 3x per week for three weeks straight, you might decide to move up to 4x per week. After moving up, you lose consistency and can't make it 4x per week for two straight weeks. Go back down to 3x per week and prove to yourself that you can be consistent, again.

I'd also like to make a point to reward your progress. It isn't great for your psyche to just torment yourself with needing to do this or needing to do that. While pain is a great motivator, affirmation and rewards also motivate.

Give yourself a sort of "joyful reward." For instance, if I finish reading a book, my reward is I get to purchase a vinyl record. I currently have a restriction of only one fried chicken meal per week. So, whenever I have fried chicken each week, that's the reward in itself (because fried chicken is one of God's many gifts to mankind). In the same way that your goals and desires need to be things you truly want, the rewards must be things you actually want. If you don't care about purchasing vinyl records, you shouldn't make it a reward. **If it's not helping you take action, it's not a good enough reward**.

Now, at a certain point, there's a line where time and life's activities collide. Let's call this the "ceiling of satisfaction." **The ceiling of satisfaction is where your consistent action toward a particular activity collides with life's other demands**. When this collision happens, we find out what level of intensity we're willing to invest into this activity. How much am I willing to commit to this activity, while still maintaining my other commitments?

This introduces the case for realistic consistency. Since most of us have been living in a life of apathy, we can't expect to climb the mountain in one day. Can you really go do a full workout every single morning before you head to work? Do you have the personal discipline to do that? Do you even have the discipline to fold your laundry that's been in the basket for multiple weeks? Ouch...that one hit too close to home. **Your ceiling of satisfaction helps you grip with the reality of what you're willing to commit to**.

Here's the really cool part, though: **the results multiply**. Your development gets better and better and better, through consistency.

"Be Fruitful, Then Multiply."

By raising the bar just slightly every week, you look back after six months, and become amazed with the progress. Then, once you've hit your ceiling of satisfaction, you just ride on the consistency of your actions. When summer hits, you've likely shattered your 20 pound goal! Take this into any other activity until you've hit that satisfying level of intensity to achieve your goals.

This will all come to fruition in stages, folks. The F6 goals I created for myself? I still work on them, and it's been over two years that I've created and edited these goals. Some things, like financial goals, were easy to map out and execute. It took me two years to make any consistent traction with my faith goals. **Please understand that you're trying to dramatically alter your outlook on life and do what only a few people do not live pathetically apathetic lives**.

Take this chapter to heart and apply it to those F6 goals of yours. Start small. Consider your circumstances.

Be fruitful, then multiply.

CHAPTER 11:

Daily Planning and Time Blocking

So, we have a list of goals and interests, correct? Great. We also understand that it's important to be fruitful, then multiply? We're on the right track. You ain't a grand master yet, though. We've only accomplished the easiest parts of converting your apathetic life into an invigorating, caring lifestyle. Doing exercises like "writing down your goals" are constantly recommended, but you should know by now that **it's meaningless unless there's consistent action that's applied.** You certainly don't want to be one of those people with a million great ideas with nothing to show for it, right? All of those great ideas are really just a distraction.

This makes me think of my old undergraduate days at Oral Roberts University, where I studied business marketing. So many business students had these lofty dreams to create innovative businesses. There's a lot of hype behind creating businesses "with a cause." It's awesome to see what businesses can do with their profits. Contributing to a charity and including givebacks with every purchase are both wonderful ways to defend a cause. Every one of us business students dreamed up ideas about creating innovative businesses and nonprofits during our time in college.

Here's the thing, **I guarantee you that 99% of us students, who had these giant dreams to create innovative organizations, social**

causes, businesses and nonprofits...never did anything (that includes me, by the way). I remember multiple startup ideas, where we had team members convinced that we could create the next men's custom-tailored clothing line. Or, how about creating a construction business that utilizes recycled plastics for low-income housing? Or, what about connecting with cashew farmers in Brazil to have them sell their products in the United States to address poverty issues in their country? Killer ideas right?

What we college students failed to see was the reality of creating a successful company like TOMS shoes. You remember TOMS, right? You buy a pair and they give a pair to someone without shoes. What does it take to actually make it a thriving business? It takes a lot of organization, a lot of research, a lot of personal investment, a lot of financial backing, a lot of sweat and tears, a lot of meetings with influential people, and a lot of YEARS of work. Actually, scratch that... DECADES of work. And, for Blake Mycoskie, the founder of TOMS shoes, this wasn't his first business. He created multiple businesses before TOMS shoes, including a laundromat for his college. You don't hear many kids dreaming about building a laundromat, huh?

When we have these "innovative" ideas, and we want to make a radical impact, our lack of work ethic inevitably kicks in. We want to take a break after an hour of studying to go to Starbucks or binge watch the next TV show. We create our list of goals and then go stop by the pool. We buy the book, but never finish reading it. There were *several* startup ideas that were bouncing around my head that never translated to anything significant.

I remember I started a couple podcasts back in college and after college. In college, my buddy and I wanted to create a comedy podcast that was about student life, current topics and other dumb ideas. We convinced a college student to do a photo shoot for us, we wrote intro music, we put together show outlines...we were making this thing as legit as possible! For one of the shows, we even sent out a survey to college students about campus love life and we were able to have over 300 people respond! Sadly, after five episodes, my teammate lost interest in the project and I didn't want to do the show by myself, so it came to a complete halt.

I would later, after college, start another podcast about state politics. It's a topic that few people are educated on and I wanted to be a not-so-boring source of information. It's amazing how impactful state politics actually are to our livelihoods and, yet, less than 30% of our US population votes in these local elections. It's hard to even find in-depth information online about local politicians! So, I ventured on. I got the same college student to do photos for free. I put together intro music, wrote up outlines, got local politicians to actually come on the podcast...I was making headway! All went well, until I missed a week, and then another week, and then got embarrassed about all the inconsistency and ended up quitting.

Being the encouraging reader you are, you think to yourself, "But, Harley, at least you went for it and gave it your best shot, right?"

I appreciate the sentiment, friend, but I must provide a knowledge bomb for you. **If you really want to make something remarkable, you invest years and years into consistently working on the craft.** My undergraduate ideas were fun to dream up and it was enjoyable to start these new things, but **it's always enjoyable to start new things.** What doomed me was that I didn't understand the necessary commitment behind any remarkable endeavor.

Daily Planning and Time Blocking

Our consulting office actually has a podcast called the Thrive Time Show Business Podcast. It earns over 500,000 downloads per month. You know what's crazy about their show? They made it there **after seven years of diligently recording episodes.** They recorded episodes every day for seven years and, finally, they reached half a million listeners per month. For a mind-blowing experience, go onto Youtube and search "Joe Rogan's first podcast episode." It looks horrible. They spent the first 10 minutes or more just trying to make the video connection work.

Here comes the capstone idea to this chapter...

I didn't understand that we MUST adequately plan out our time on a consistent basis. We must always be specific and intentional with how our time is spent. People are so ready to say that the day is unpredictable, or it's always "up in the air." Again, we grant grace for everyone's failed intentions because everyone collectively misses the mark on their goals. "Well at least you tried!" - says everyone who constantly can't figure out how to make great things happen in life.

News flash, if you don't "seize your time," as Napoleon Hill puts it, and determine how you spend your time every single day, time will find you years down the road wondering where it went. **Do you really want to be another old geezer that looks back at life and wonders where time has gone by?** Nir Eyal, whose writing appears in publications like *Fast Company, Harvard Business Review* and *The Atlantic*, writes,

> *"Only by setting aside specific time in our schedules for traction (the action that draws us toward what we want in life) can we turn our backs on distraction. **Without planning ahead, it's impossible to tell the difference between traction and distraction.**"*

Pathetically Apathetic

We can't expect these great things to happen without being immensely intentional. So, it's time to break out the calendar and block out what your day looks like. I don't care if you use the calendar on your phone, Google calendar, a daily planner book, a print out calendar or a scratch sheet of paper. **Just write down what your day looks like, every single day.**

Daily Planning and Time Blocking

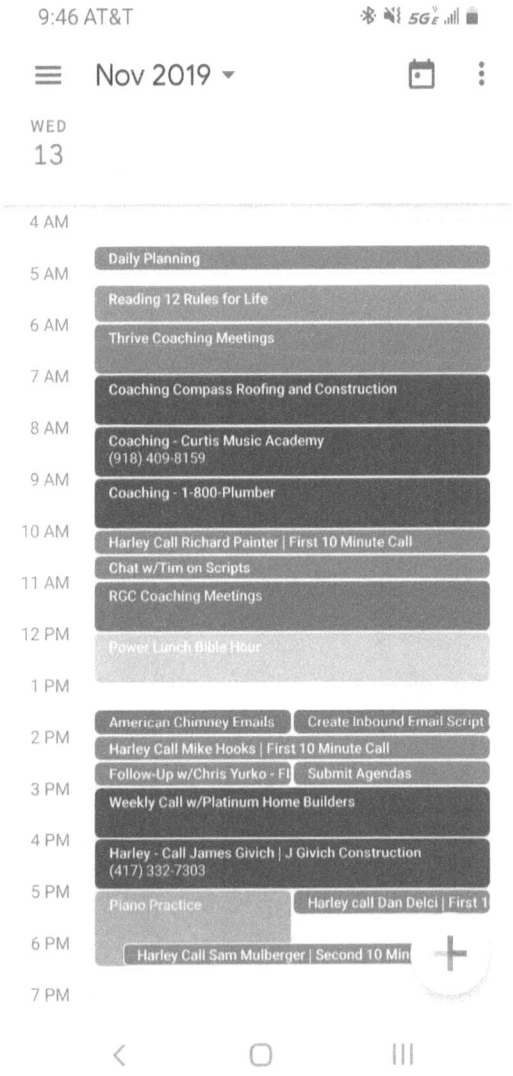

(This was Wednesday, November 13th, 2019.)

Pathetically Apathetic

You've got a day of work ahead of you, correct? Well, what are you going to do on that workday? What will you do before work? How about during lunch? Will you do anything during lunch? What about after work? Do you like to do certain activities after work? Are there certain things you should do after work? How do you spend your time on the weekends? What would you like to do during the weekends? Get out the calendar and map out your day. Curious to know what this looks like? I shared an example of my work schedule in a previous chapter, but here's a snapshot of my calendar again on page 206:

You and I have various things that need to get done in our days. In order to get them accomplished, they need to get done at a specific time. How will I remember when meetings happen? I schedule it in the calendar. When do I actually have the time to take care of action items? I schedule the action items in the calendar. If I want to make headway in a book I'm reading, but I have a full day of work, when can I read? I schedule it in the calendar. The goal here, as Nir Eyal puts it, *"is to eliminate all white space on your calendar so you're left with a template for how you intend to spend your time each day."* And, don't worry, this calendar didn't look like this at 5am when I planned my day (see Daily Planning as an event at 4:30 am). On November 13th, I had one client cancel their meeting and I added five action items throughout the day. There were also some action items I ended up not completing. How could I possibly keep up with this schedule in my head? You can't! **That's why you plan it out and assign times on the calendar.** There's just NO WAY you can remember everything in your head.

But, how do I remember all the random, important things that occur throughout the day? **I also create a printed out to-do list each day for what activities need to be done**. Here's what my to-do list looked like on November 13th, 2019, on page 208:

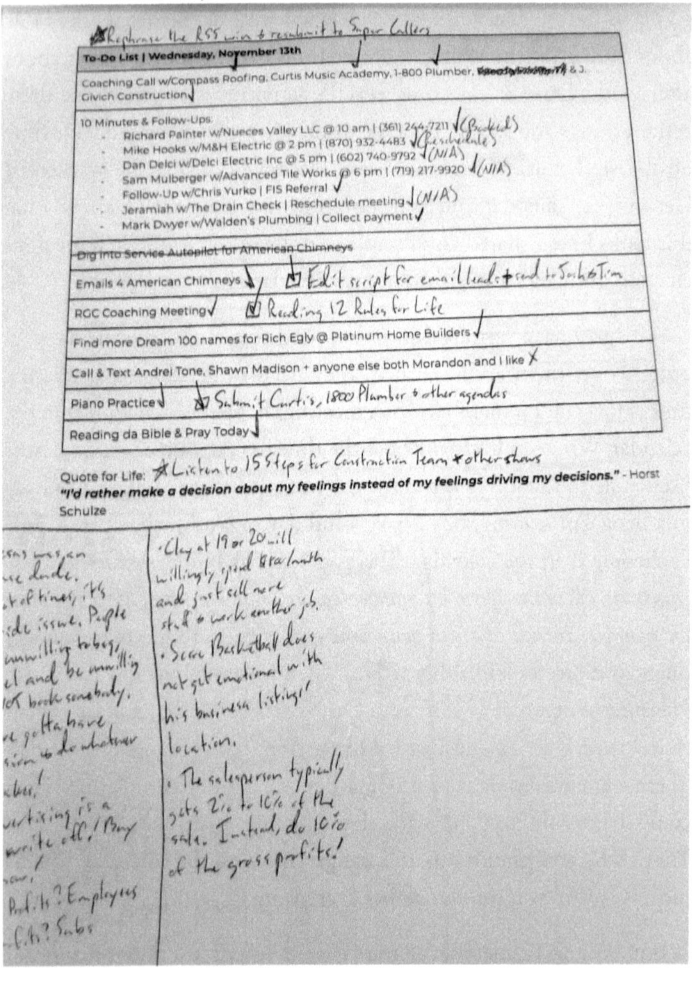

Daily Planning and Time Blocking

> **To-Do List | Wednesday, November 13th**
>
> ✱ Rephrase the RSS win & resubmit to Super Callers
>
> Coaching Call w/Compass Roofing, Curtis Music Academy, 1-800 Plumber, ~~Beauty Boutique (?)~~ & J. Givich Construction
>
> 10 Minutes & Follow-Ups:
> - Richard Painter w/Nueces Valley LLC @ 10 am | (361) 244-7211 ✓ (Rescheduled)
> - Mike Hooks w/M&H Electric @ 2 pm | (870) 932-4483 ✓ (Rescheduled)
> - Dan Delci w/Delci Electric Inc @ 5 pm | (602) 740-9792 ✓ (N/A)
> - Sam Mulberger w/Advanced Tile Works @ 6 pm | (719) 217-9920 ✓ (N/A)
> - Follow-Up w/Chris Yurko | FIS Referral ✓
> - Jeramiah w/The Drain Check | Reschedule meeting ✓ (N/A)
> - Mark Dwyer w/Walden's Plumbing | Collect payment ✓
>
> ~~Dig into Service Autopilot for American Chimneys~~
>
> Emails 4 American Chimneys ✓ ☐ Edit script for email leads + send to Josh & Tim
>
> RGC Coaching Meeting ✓ ☐ Reading 12 Rules for Life
>
> Find more Dream 100 names for Rich Egly @ Platinum Home Builders ✓
>
> Call & Text Andrei Tone, Shawn Madison + anyone else both Morandon and I like ✗
>
> Piano Practice ☐ Submit Curtis, 1800 Plumber + other agendas
>
> Reading da Bible & Pray Today ✓
>
> Quote for Life: ✱ Listen to 15 Steps for Construction Team + other shows
> **"I'd rather make a decision about my feelings instead of my feelings driving my decisions."** - Horst Schulze

---

[handwritten notes, left column:]
...sas was, an
...de dude.
...t of times, it's
...side issue. People
...unwilling to beg,
...el and be unwilling
...to book somebody.
...gotta have
...sion to do whatever
...else!
...vertising is a
...write off. / Buy
...now,
Profits? Employees
...its? Subs

[handwritten notes, right column:]
- Guy at 19 or 20 will willingly spend $8k a month and just sell more stuff or work another job.
- Sean Basketball does not get emotional with his business listings / location.
- The salesperson typically gets 2% to 10% of the sale. Instead, do 10% of the gross profits.

(My to-do list for Wednesday, November 13th, 2019.)

It details all the action items in my day. I will have meetings with notes and additional action items to address. The checkmarks tell me that the action item or the meeting was completed. Stars tell me that I should look into this later or get it done later. X's symbolize that I didn't get it done and I didn't really need to get it done.

You may notice that I'm using pen and paper for my to-do list. Statista, a digital marketing research organization, shares that adults spend an average of 144 minutes a day on social media alone. According to Pew Research, *"Roughly half (54%) believe they spend too much time on their cell phone, while 41% say they spend too much time on social media."* Of parents surveyed in the U.K., 46% said they "feel addicted" to their mobile devices. In 2015, the average person received approximately 64 phone notifications per day. Studies have shown that people with their phones in another room "significantly outperformed" those who had their phones on the desk, and did slightly better than those who had their phones in a pocket. **We need to intentionally find ways off the smartphone.** So, yes, I print out a to-do list.

Now, you may look at my calendar, see the various calendar events and the to-do list to match the day and think, "Holy...that looks crazy overwhelming." I want to encourage you that **there's really only one activity that MUST HAPPEN in order to make this whole thing possible...daily planning.** Determine when you will build a plan for your day, every day. No exceptions. Block out time for each activity. Stick to the calendar as best as possible. Those are the steps.

You will not succeed immediately. Similar to skateboarding for the first time, it's going to be awkward and you'll have some abrupt, painful falls. People will throw different activities onto your plan that you didn't expect. You'll get caught up talking to someone and realize that you were supposed to start laundry. Now, it's already time to leave

Daily Planning and Time Blocking

for dinner, so...I guess no laundry? Or maybe I stay up late tonight doing laundry? **You'll also realize how long things actually take.** Does it really take just 30 minutes to do groceries? Or does it take an hour because of drive time and the fact that you never remember where the aisle for rice is?

Are there days when a calendar and to-do list isn't necessary? Only on days where you don't want to get stuff done. The Roman philosopher, Seneca the Younger, said two thousand years ago, *"People are frugal in guarding their personal property; but as soon as it comes to squandering time, they are most wasteful of the one thing in which it is right to be stingy."* You just wrote down all of those great goals for your family, faith, finances, fitness, friends and fun, right? WHEN WILL YOU DO THESE THINGS!?

Write it down. Plan your time every single day, before the day starts. Follow the calendar. Repeat.

As you block out your time and create your to-do list of action items, you'll become a freak of nature to most people. They'll look at your calendar and gasp for dear life. They will be concerned about your well-being and sanity. How should you respond? Embrace it. This is the normal mode for any ridiculously successful and intentional person. This methodology is run by anyone who wants to make something of their lives. Anyone who plans out their time, and honors their calendar, gets stuff done. With many days, weeks, months and years of consistent implementation, you will suddenly realize how far you've gone and be proud of yourself.

Pathetically Apathetic

Pitfalls to Watch For

But, I must say, most people already know this stuff is important. They know that using a calendar is a good thing. They understand that creating to-do lists is helpful. Again, I'll remind you that nothing is revolutionary or new in this book. There are some common pitfalls, which ultimately, thwart anyone from doing these simple activities consistently. I'd like to quickly address these situations and provide you with steps to overcome them.

1. **It Sounds Impossible.** When you read that one of my bosses diligently recorded podcasts every single day for seven years, it likely provoked an audible gasp of disbelief. *Every day? For seven years?? What…?? Didn't anything get in the way of recording a show? What about vacations???* We're so used to unplanned interruptions and taking breaks that planning our time effectively sounds impossible.

    So, here's what you do. **Just think about today, every day.** In Matthew 6:34, Jesus provides some holy insight. *"So don't worry about tomorrow, for tomorrow will bring its own worries. Today's trouble is enough for today."* **Do not be overwhelmed by the magnitude of great people. They all started where you're starting.** Just plan for today, every day. You will get better, trust me.

Daily Planning and Time Blocking

2. **No One Knows How to Plan Their Time or Where to Start.** Nir Eyal, the best-selling author of the book, *Indistractable*, shares research from PPAI that, *"only a third of Americans keep a daily schedule, which means the vast majority wake up every morning with no formal plans."* Even if we write down to-do lists or say that we "rely on our calendar," Nir continues to give some perspective. *"We write down all the things we want to do and hope we'll find the time throughout the day to do them. Unfortunately this method has some serious flaws."* The keyword is we "hope" to find the time.

   Well, congratulations, now you know! It really is this simple. There isn't an app that makes time management more magical. There aren't hacks, tips or tricks that finally break people from dysfunction. Just plan your day, every single day. Block times in the calendar for every important activity. Print out a paper to-do list to track your progress throughout the day. **There is nothing else you need to add.**

3. **You Don't Understand How it Works.** You're not a tech-savvy person, you haven't done this before, your environment is dysfunctional, yeah, we get it, this won't be easy. **Shut up and just figure it out!** Force a young person to teach you how Google calendar works. Fire idiots who work in your company. Kick out dysfunctional family members who shouldn't be in your life. **You cannot afford to**

let your environment determine how successful your life will be. Please, read chapter 6 again to get a thorough reminder of this.

4. **It Sounds Too Intense and Anal.** Just go ahead and read chapter 5 again, and you'll be reminded that the people who truly make things happen sound "too intense." They sound like the anal, detail-oriented kid that makes everyone look stupid. But, in fact, we need more of these kids in our lives to create remarkable things. We need you to be remarkable. I'll let Seth Godin, the blogger who was on *TIME Magazine*'s 25 best blogs of 2009 list, give you the thorough motivation to get your ass in gear.

    *"'Life's too short' is repeated often enough to be a cliché, but this time it's true. You don't have enough time to be both unhappy and mediocre. It's not just pointless, it's painful. **Instead of wondering when your next vacation is, maybe you ought to set up a life you don't need to escape from.**"*

The steps are simple. Now, it's time to deal with the hard, rewarding questions to illuminate what you truly care about doing with your life. Here's the most important question to ask as you write out your goals, plan your days and make your goals a reality... **what will you be satisfied with?**

Daily Planning and Time Blocking

CHAPTER 12:

What Will You Be Satisfied With?

What if you never accomplished the goals you had in mind? Would you still be satisfied with how you lived your life?

"Where Do You See Yourself in Five Years" is Annoying

As you block out your time to effectively go after your goals, you'll begin to see further and further down the road. You'll begin to map out what next year will look like and, even, what the next decade looks like. Before you bought this book, a lot of questions were swirling around your head. What do I actually want to do with my life? What do I genuinely care about? Where do you see yourself in the next year? Where do you see yourself in the next five years?

The "where do you see yourself" question still irritates me. Who can legitimately answer this question? No one can confidently say what the heck their lives will be like in five years. And, if you gave a confident answer, how do you know that what you predict will happen? It's a question with practically zero genuine confidence attached to it.

You may have come this far in the book and still haven't found out what you want in life. Even while writing this book, I'm still tossing and turning. You could be 25 years old, like me, or 50 years old, and still deal with this same lurking question.

We've got many years ahead of us...how should we spend them?

Some will say to live every day like it's your last. Steve Jobs apparently asked himself this question each morning: *"If today were the last day of my life, would I want to do what I am about to do today?"* Ray Charles, the famous blind pianist, agrees. He says, *"Live each day like it's your last, 'cause one day you gonna be right."*

The way I see it, this question isn't helpful. It's easy for Ray Charles to say this, because he's Ray Charles. Ray Charles and others who have "found their calling," can tell us this advice, because they actually spent their last days doing exactly what they loved. I don't know about you, but I'd feel pretty hopeless if I were told to "live like it's my last day." I wouldn't want to work at my job. That's what I do all day. I'd probably see my family one last time? I don't want to see my family all day, every day, though. See how this advice can be annoying?

I'd rather, as a random blogger I found on the Internet described, live like it's my first day. He writes.

> *"Living like today is your first day on Earth opens you up to all possibilities, has no pre-loaded expectations or desires to fill, with no framework for past regrets or anxiety about the future."*
>
> - Joshua Bradley, a blogger I found on Medium.com

Pathetically Apathetic

This still doesn't answer our first big question, though. What the hell do we want to do with all this time!? I've been able to actually answer this question more and more. **After a record of consistency and diligence toward aspirations, my sight becomes clearer.** I accurately assess where I invest my time and, based on that, I can determine how realistic the accomplishment of my goals will be. Instead of making up hypothetical answers to "where I see myself in five years," I can give concrete answers like…

1. I will continue to create musical projects with piano, either in classical music or jazz music.
2. I will continue to read books.
3. I will continue to work 40+ hours per week, every week.
4. I will continue to save $500 per month towards my Roth IRA to ensure that I can retire easily.
5. I will continue to workout every single week and maintain running endurance (sub-7-minute mile and 14-minute 2 miles).
6. I will make other monetary investments along the way to build more wealth.
7. I will continue to go to Church and profess to be a Christian.
8. I will continue to write, because I've found over the last several years, I keep coming back to this activity. Might as well commit and become very good at it.

Are there some things I'd like to say about my future? Absolutely. I'd love to say that I finally gained 15 to 20 extra pounds of muscle and I'm known as a really fit guy. I'd love to say that I'll be married in five years…maybe even have a kid! I'd love to say that, in five years, I'll have found a city to truly call home and officially plant lifelong roots. I'd love to say that in five years, I'll be a full-time ghostwriter.

What Will You Be Satisfied With?

I can't accurately say those things, though. **I haven't seen my actions prove the validity of these dreams.** It's no reason to lose hope in myself, but it would be wrong for me to declare with full confidence any of these goals. My history shows that I haven't cared enough to diet and exercise consistently enough to see dramatic changes. Due to the lack of romantic relationships I've had, I can't confidently say that I'll find a wife in five years. I can't confidently say that, in five years, ghostwriting will be my main career priority. I can't say that ghostwriting, or writing in general, will effectively fund my life. In fact, I can't confidently say that I'll ever be able to totally fund my financial goals with writing. **That's a scary thought: to willingly pursue a goal that you may never fully accomplish?** Seems a little crazy.

In reality, we have no idea whether anything we plan or do will come to fruition. We could die tomorrow! Some illness could take us out, a car accident from a drunk driver could permanently cripple us. Our priorities could dramatically change if, let's say, the health of your father drops drastically and you know you're the only one to provide consistent care to him. You could think that these things will never happen. I mean, really, what are the chances!? But, I must ask, **what will you be satisfied with?**

Pathetically Apathetic

A Desperate Plea to Deal With Reality (i.e. Trade-Offs)

After you've gone through a few wrestling matches with yourself to narrow your focus, you'll begin to notice that **there are really only a few things you actually care about doing long-term.** There are only a few things you are willing to consistently do for the rest of your life. Rather than jumping here or there with your ambitions, goals and passions, you'll find certain activities hit the sweet spot. It's a sweet spot that always keeps giving. You may not always be pumped up and jovial about these activities, but you'll never grow tired of doing them.

That, to me, is playing piano and writing. My interest never dwindles, and I'm never "done" with these activities. I'll never really reach a final destination with them, and I love that. I'm willing to do these two things for the rest of my life. But, as you can imagine, these two activities don't guarantee financial success. They are creative activities and, typically, anything creative comes with few opportunities for financial success. While I'm reassured by one of my bosses that ghostwriting can create a legitimate career for me, I still don't hear many people preaching about the "job security" of writing.

Your job may not be one of your satisfying life-long activities. As I write this book, I'm still working at my consulting job and waking up at 4:30 am, at the latest, every day. That's Monday through Friday devoted to that job. For some people, it would be quite rewarding to help business owners reach their financial and time-related goals. For whatever reason, the work doesn't provide me with deep, emotional satisfaction. Is it a job with fabulous people in the office? Oh yeah, we've got great people at the job. Does it pay well? I definitely earn enough to save and satisfy my current needs. If I stayed at the job long-term, would I make more money? Guaranteed.

What Will You Be Satisfied With?

Do I want to do consulting for the rest of my life? Nope, not at all. Here's a trade-off question that will help you with your desired goals... are you willing to be poor and spend all of your time mastering these unique activities? Or do you want to provide for your home financially, while still blocking out time for these unique activities?

Take a moment and consider what I just asked.

Are you willing to work enough to put food on the table and provide shelter, while also spending your own unpaid time advancing in the craft you truly care about? Even if the work you do isn't your great, lifelong ambition, is that okay with you? Personally, I vote to keep myself out of poverty. On the other hand, lots of people are willing to suffer for several years in poverty while they make their great ambition work. Robert Caro, the multi-Pulitzer Prize winning author, has spoken out several times in interviews about how, during his first book, *The Power Broker*, his wife sold the house without his knowledge to keep food on the table. **They scraped by, for eight years, in poverty while he devoted his life to this first book about Robert Moses. This book went on to be his 1st Pulitzer Prize-winning book.**

While these are the stories we hear in interviews, podcasts, television shows, Youtube channels and books like this one, please realize this is the exception! **What if Robert Caro went on to publish this book and his writing sucked?** He did have several years under his belt as an investigative journalist and he did spend eight years slaving away at this book. Is that a guarantee it'll be good, though? It could've been a great book, but MANY great books are hardly ever read. Then, what would have been the result of those eight years of poverty? These are some troubling thoughts.

The longer I live, the more I hear about negative life moments.

Marriages falling apart. Businesses failing. Diseases ruining lives. People committing suicide. Families continually in financial burden. Accidents causing death or crippling injuries. Do I really want to spend all my days honing my craft in piano, making just enough to get by, when so much could happen? Call me "alarmist," but I'd rather be prepared. **I'd rather know that I can put food on the table than bank on becoming the next Ray Charles.**

These are the tough trade-offs that truly test your desires. What will you be satisfied with? So, you really want to learn a musical instrument, huh? You want to be so good that you play live gigs and actually get paid to be a musician? You want to form a band who plays together regularly on the weekends? You want to get so good that you start touring and sign with a label? Well…you've gotta live and pay the bills somehow! That means you need to find a job and work your butt off on nights and weekends with the band. That means you probably need to say "no" to TV, to social media and to those Tuesday night hangouts you used to go to. That means you may become a pariah so your excellence with the band can be realized.

This is why it's important to figure out what you'll be satisfied with. Would it be awesome if I could sell out theaters playing music for thousands of fans? Yeah, that would be really cool! Have I come to grips with the fact that I won't drop my current work obligations, live in poverty and see if I can "hit it big?" I have. Am I content with this reality? Yes, I am. Have I set up an alternate goal that I'm more confident I can achieve? Yes I have. Will it still require me to practice three to four hours each week, every week to attain this goal in a timely manner? Yes it will. Do I also understand that this "timely manner" could be as long as a four year period, or more? I knew this before starting my first lesson.

What Will You Be Satisfied With?

What are the results of asking these tough questions and resolving to be content with my reality? I can live happily satisfied and genuinely impressed with my own progress. **It's amazing how my music teacher tells me how quickly I'm learning this material, when really, I've just been doing the same thing ever since starting. Three hours, every week. That's it.**

What about writing this book? **It means that all of my writing needs to occur on weekends and evenings and early mornings, while I'm not at the office.** Because, if I want to make sure I can pay the bills and continue to save 30% of my income, I need to keep thriving at my job! I wouldn't be thriving at my job if I skipped meetings with clients and dropped the ball on my action items! The 100 hours it took me to create the 1st draft for this book were spent outside of my work obligations.

Well, actually, I got curious about whether it legitimately took me 100 hours to write the 1st draft of this book. It turns out, I wrote the 1st draft in UNDER 100 hours! After investigating how I blocked out my time in the calendar, here are the statistics on what it took to write the 1st draft of this book:

1. The total amount of time spent writing the 1st draft? 80 hours
2. I started writing outlines for the book on August 31st, 2019. I finished the 1st draft on December 28th, 2019. **So it took me approximately four months to write the 1st draft.**
3. These hours did not include time spent reading books or listening to interviews during the four month period. There were likely more than 80 hours that contributed to the 1st draft.

4. I only spent 30 days actually working on the book.
Whether it was one hour or 6 ½ hours in a day, I interacted with the 1st draft on 30 separate days. So, technically, I could have finished my 1st draft in one month.

How could I possibly look back almost a year in the past and find accurate numbers on how and when I spent my time? I did the five steps all the way back in chapter one! Need a reminder?

First Step: Specifically identify all the things you want to solve. My specific thing I wanted to solve was writing the 1st draft of this book.

Second Step: Find out how to solve the problems you just wrote down. How do I write the 1st draft of my book? Well...you kind of just start writing. You put together an outline plan of how you think the chapters should break down, but you just have to START WRITING!

Third Step: Schedule when and how frequently you will take action. From writing outlines to reading articles to referencing books and interviews to proofreading so I don't sound like a complete idiot, **everything needs to be scheduled in a calendar!** Honestly, I wasn't exactly sure when I wanted to get this 1st draft done. As it got closer to the end of the year and as I continued to make headway, I realized that a great goal would be to finish the first draft by the end of 2019. To ensure that I actually finish the book by the end of 2019, I execute the third step again and again.

Fourth Step: Honor your calendar. How does it benefit me to schedule blocks in my calendar to work on the book and then NOT work on the book? This is when I tell myself motivating, encouraging comments like, "Harley, don't be an idiot and lie to yourself. Honor your calendar."

What Will You Be Satisfied With?

Fifth Step: Repeat.

That's it.

You're Still Remarkable, No Matter What You Decide

I would argue that it's so easy nowadays to be remarkably awesome. Do you have a healthy marriage with great kids that behave? Do you work at a job that you actually enjoy? Does that job give you enough income to pay for vacations and allow you to adequately save for retirement? Are you healthy with your physical fitness and don't face limiting physical issues? Do you volunteer your time and contribute to help out your community in a positive way? News flash, you are remarkably awesome compared to the vast majority of people on Earth. Good job, you.

And, if this isn't you, be encouraged that doing the steps in this book WILL make you remarkable. Who the hell actually uses a calendar this effectively?? Who is intentional with how they use their time? Who plans out their day and blocks out time to execute their most important activities? Who says "no" to things all the time because it conflicts with their personal schedule? Who writes down their goals and breaks down how they can actually achieve those goals on a weekly basis? Who's actually consistent with their disciplines and commitments? The more and more people I talk to, the more and more I realize that nobody does these things. Heck, I didn't do this before my consulting job! **I lived for 23 years as a pathetically apathetic human.**

What will you be satisfied with? Only you can be the judge of that. What this book should do is wake you up to being intentional with all the time you have.

Pathetically Apathetic

Think about your death bed. I brought up this hypothetical situation earlier, but it helps clear up what you truly care about accomplishing. **If you were on your deathbed and you looked back on your life, what would really disappoint you if you didn't learn or do something?**

(On your deathbed, thinking about what you wish happened)

If you really wanted to blaze a career helping to drill wells in Africa, why don't you apply to serve or work at the current organizations who do this? I mean, literally, if you just type into Google, "organizations that drill wells," you'll find plenty of people to send applications to. If they don't respond, don't stop harassing them. Show up at their freakin' door if you have to and say, "Hey, I want to work with you and I'm willing to do it for free. Please, LET ME HELP!"

What this book should hopefully sparks in your brain cells is the decision to figure out what will satisfy you.

If you really wanted to make your career digging wells in Africa, you would find a way. You would slave in your current job for years

What Will You Be Satisfied With?

and build a storehouse of cash for savings. You would research about digging wells and figure out what these current organizations look for in job applicants. You would improve your personal knowledge and skills to go above and beyond what they look for. You would find a way to move to the city that the organization is based in or move to the village in Africa where these wells are actually built. If you really wanted it, you would do whatever is necessary to make it happen.

My consulting firm actually has multiple people who offered to work for free to prove their worth. One of them was a website developer that didn't have a ton of knowledge or experience doing the work, but he knew how dominant our organization was. So, he worked for free for almost a month before getting his first paid hours. He's still at the company after seven years and is now our lead website developer.

What will you be satisfied with? If you have big goals for your future, but you know you need to put in time right now to focus on more pressing issues…you should probably do that. I'll quote Dr. Peterson again to really hit home the point. He writes:

> *"Don't blame capitalism, the radical left, or the iniquity of your enemies. Don't reorganize the state until you have ordered your own experience. Have some humility.* ***If you cannot bring peace to your household, how dare you try to rule a city?"***

Dale Carnegie gave this similar knowledge bomb back in 1936, 26 years before Dr. Peterson was born. He writes:

Pathetically Apathetic

"Do you know someone you would like to change and regulate and improve? Good! That is fine. I am all in favor of it, but why not begin on yourself? From a purely selfish standpoint, that is a lot more profitable than trying to improve others - yes, and a lot less dangerous."

You can still be remarkable. Most aren't remarkable. Seth Godin is one of the premier voices in the marketing world. He's written 18 best-selling books, and has one of the most popular blogs on the planet, with over 600,000 visitors/month ("seth.blog" is the domain). In one of his best-selling books, *Purple Cow*, one of his biggest themes breaks down how pivotal it is to be remarkable in a sea of marketing. We're presented with so many advertisements and messages to buy this and buy that…it just doesn't make sense for businesses to present average or expected products or services.

Yet, most business owners still do, because standing out in a crowd is risky. You get unauthorized attention when you paint your work truck bright pink. You get heckled whenever you try a racy joke on stage and it's not done well. You get criticized for bringing up alternative points of view at your family dinner table. It's "safe" to provide what's expected.

Seth would argue that what's expected should be challenged. Follow the new rule that Seth communicates here:

"The old rule was this: CREATE SAFE, ORDINARY PRODUCTS AND COMBINE THEM WITH GREAT MARKETING. The new rule is: CREATE REMARKABLE PRODUCTS THAT THE RIGHT PEOPLE SEEK OUT."

How does this apply to you, the people who don't have a business? **You can easily be remarkable with your career.** When you read that 70% of people hate their jobs and 53% of all employees are disengaged

What Will You Be Satisfied With?

in the workplace, it should provide a wide-open doorway for you to excel. Here are some very simple ways you can seize the opportunity to be brilliant in your company:

1. **Get to work earlier than everyone else and leave later than everyone else.** Don't do it once or twice. Do it all the time.

2. If the trash is full, **take out the trash**. Don't leave these simple cleaning duties to the "maid crew."

3. **Smile more.** As quoted in *How to Win Friends and Influence People*, *"I have known people who succeeded because they have a rip-roaring good time conducting their business. Later, I saw those people change as the fun became work. The business had grown dull. They lost all joy in it, and they failed."*

4. Be the guy or girl with a ready compliment or positive remark about other people. As it's also stated in *How to Win Friends and Influence People*, *"**Be hearty in your approbation and lavish in your praise**, and people will cherish your words and treasure them and repeat them over a lifetime - repeating them years after you have forgotten them."*

If you just do these four things in your career and NEVER STOP, you will become remarkable within a year. You will get promotions. You will find better friends. You will attract better prospects for dating and marriage. You will accomplish your goals much more quickly than you could imagine.

Pathetically Apathetic

If you're worried about getting criticized for suddenly being nice or making these changes in your habits, I will refer you back to one of the best quotes I've ever read by Seth Godin in *Purple Cow*.

> *"If you're remarkable, it's likely that some people won't like you. That's part of the definition of remarkable.* **Nobody gets unanimous praise–ever. The best the timid can hope for is to be unnoticed. Criticism comes to those who stand out."**

In case you need a Godly man to tell you a similar knowledge bomb, here's Pastor T.D. Jakes:

> *"Exceptional and ordinary always have a conflict. Anytime exceptional people dwell in the midst of ordinary thinking people there's always going to be conflict."*

We, as people who have decided to become exceptional, will always have tension with the ordinary. Those who settle for lackluster will bring you down to their level, if you let them.

Good bosses will always hire people of excellence. Excellence is so rare. I'm really coming in hot with all of these great quotes, but Steve Jobs plainly states that, **"Some people just aren't used to an environment where excellence is expected."** If you've been excellent and you KNOW that you've been excellent...yet nothing has changed or improved about your work life in years, why are you still working at this job?? MOVE! Go somewhere that expects excellence and appreciates excellence. They will compensate you well in due time.

The great action step to take here is to **identify what you'll truly be satisfied with.** Determine a timeframe for when you'd like to get these things done. Does this activity need to be accomplished in the next year? In the next month? What will it take for you to get it

What Will You Be Satisfied With?

accomplished in that timeframe? Maybe you can push it off for five years because, right now, you need to focus on something else.

There are no wrong decisions here. The only wrong decision is to continue to live in cognitive dissonance, to continue to talk about achieving such grandiose goals and, yet, still take zero action towards them.

I wouldn't be satisfied with that, and you shouldn't be either.

CHAPTER 13:

Stop Waiting for the Right Moment

I'll keep this last chapter short since you've actually finished a book this year. You're part of only 19% of all Americans who actually read for pleasure on any given day, according to a report by the *Washington Post*. Good job.

For the last time, here's the main message. People continually live with cognitive dissonance. They don't feel like they have command over what happens and, therefore, live each day thinking it could be better. We aren't caring enough about being intentional with our lives. We're apathetic about making dramatic improvements to our lives or the lives of others. So, we settle. We complain. We blame other parties, people and groups for our "victimhood" mentality.

While you may very well be the victim of unfortunate circumstances, this is no reason to mope around and whine. Take action! Fix the issues around you and care about improving your life circumstances. Look to the many great leaders and influencers of our time. They all came from similar, if not worse situations than you. **Will it be challenging? Only the most important things are.**

What are the particular action steps, again? I'll list them out for a thorough review.

Stop Waiting for the Right Moment

1. List out all of your goals, your desires, your ambitions and everything you'd love to accomplish. Get it ALL in writing. Pen and paper will do, but I suggest grabbing a big whiteboard.

2. Write out everything you currently do with your time. What takes up your time on a weekly basis?

3. Then, after writing everything out on a paper pad or marker board, begin to **block out your time on a calendar.** For now, put on a calendar what you're currently doing. I like Google calendar (calendar.google.com/), but you can use a lot of different calendar planning tools. Paper still works well too. You can print off a week-long calendar and fill in the blanks.

> a. This only works well if you **prioritize your daily planning** time. When will you sit down, eliminate all distractions, and think about nothing else except planning your day? Don't get any to-do list items knocked out during this time. **You simply think about when you will get to-do list items done during your day.**
>
> b. Based on your daily planning time, **BLOCK OUT the time slots in your calendar for when you will focus on activities in your day.** This applies to EVERYTHING in your life. Hanging out with the family? Block it out. Practicing piano? Block it out. Reading a book? Block it out. Picking up the mail? Block it out. Telling your wife you love her? Block it out. I'm serious.

4. On top of blocking out time in your calendar, it would behoove you to also **create your to-do list for each day.** Having a written list of all your action items

helps to free you from needing to remember every little thing. Plus, you'll add items to your plate throughout your day, or get it done tomorrow when you block out the time for it the next morning.

5. You can also **print off your calendar for the day**, which will free you from even needing your phone. Our smartphones are proven, with study upon study, to be a pivotal force of distraction in our lives. By printing off your calendar and to-do list, you will remove the need to check your phone!

6. As you get better and better at time-blocking your life, **break down your goals and interests into bite-size chunks.** So, you want to learn a new language, correct? Well, what are the first steps you need to take? Download Duolingo or some other language service and schedule time to practice this new language. How much time can you take each week, based on your current schedule, to learn this new language? How quickly do you want to learn it? There's a tremendous difference between one hour per week and four hours per week. You'll likely learn the language 4x faster with four hours per week! **What will you be satisfied with?**

7. Over time, you'll **determine which activities you need to care about and which ones you need to say "no" to.** You'll discover this through trial and error. You will only know what you truly care about with action. Words can only satisfy for so long.

Stop Waiting for the Right Moment

Never stop doing this. Diligence is one of the rarest things to master. Most people don't have it and, when they do, it only lasts for a brief period. To have the diligence to do something every week? For years? That means you've figured out what you truly care about and are no longer tolerating apathy in your life. You are intentional with how you live, and you're committed to living a life of excellence for the long haul.

Please do not expect this to radically transform your life overnight. I can't say it enough, but I'm convinced that nothing truly impactful happens in one evening or a single moment. It's either a culmination of various events that leads to a dramatic moment, or it's the consistent implementation of good action that causes great results.

Now, all this being said, here are some stumbling blocks you will likely encounter as you implement these steps into your life:

1. Your Friends, Family Members, Colleagues at Work, and Every Other Human on the Planet Will Think You're Weird.

   a. You'll become tremendously focused and people don't usually like that. Find better people.

   b. People will throw at you other responsibilities, activities and tasks that *sound good*, but only distract you from your focused goals. You'll experience brief pain when saying "no," but the decision will provide lots of joy.

2. You Will Ask Yourself Really Harsh Questions About the Goals You Wrote Down.

   a. Don't take yourself lightly. This is your life we're talking about.

3. You Will Consistently Fail at Being Consistent, Until You Don't.

    a. It's a process of growth and development. Expect to fix yourself over a lifetime. Bank on the long game. You won't disappoint yourself that way.

4. You Might Get Bored With the Simplicity of it All.

    a. Doing new things is fun. Doing the same things over and over again? Boring at first, until you find out what you really enjoy doing. Then it becomes fun building this simple, regular lifestyle.

5. If You Don't Fully Embrace This Strategy, It Won't Work Well.

    a. Don't half-ass this. It's not supposed to be easy. You're missing the point. Just shut up and do it.

6. Listen to More and More Voices of Wisdom.

    a. Please do not lean on your own intuition. The only reason I'm here and I've been able to do what I currently do is by listening and applying what I've learned from hundreds of conversations and interviews with great people. Find mentors. Tune into podcasts. Watch interviews with the greatest people on Earth. Never stop listening to wisdom.

Trust me. The longer you do this, the more you will identify these undeniable correlations and truths about life. Ladies and gentlemen, good luck. It's time for you to enjoy where your life is headed.

Books to Read After This Book

- *Think and Grow Rich* by Napoleon Hill
- *How to Win Friends and Influence People* by Dale Carnegie
- *Indistractable* by Nir Eyal
- *12 Rules for Life* by Dr. Jordan Peterson
- *Fight for the Forgotten* by Justin Wren
- *The Millionaire Next Door* by Stanley and Danko
- *Leadership and Self-Deception* by The Arbinger Institute
- *When Helping Hurts* by Corbett and Fikkert
- *The Happiness Project* by Gretchen Rubin
- *Mastery* by Robert Greene

Stop being apathetic. Start caring about what you want to do and where you want your life to go. Because right now, most of the world is pathetically apathetic. It's about time you weren't.

Did You Enjoy This Book?

I'm very glad you enjoyed this book! The best way you can illustrate to me that this book was impactful to you is by living it. Implement the simple steps and come back to me in three months. How can you get a hold of me?

- Find me on my website: www.harleywrites.com

- Find me on social medias like Facebook and Instagram

- Why Would You Reach Out?
    a. To tell me about your experience with *Pathetically Apathetic*

    b. To have me help you write a book

    c. To have me play piano for you

    d. To have a non-specific friend

- If you need a person to reach out to for some extra guidance, feel free to reach out to me! Give me a call at (972) 207-3100. If I don't answer the phone call, shoot me a text message with your name and why you'd like to talk. You can also shoot me an email (harley.liechty@gmail.com).

Sources

An Introduction to Apathy

- *"In research conducted by Patrick Heck, a social psychologist, he finds that 65% of Americans believe they are above average in intelligence."* - Patrick R. Heck and others, PLOS ONE, July 3, 2018, https://journals.plos.org/plosone/article?id=10.1371/journal.pone.0200103

- *"According to a 2016 journal titled, "The Illusion of Moral Superiority," psychologists from the University of London concluded…"* - Ben M. Tappin & Ryan T. McKay, SAGE Journals, October 19, 2016, https://journals.sagepub.com/doi/full/10.1177/1948550616673878?legid=spspp%3B194855061 6673878v1&patientinform-links=yes

- *""The Bias Blindspot" research article conducted by Stanford University, revealed…"* - Emily Pronin, SAGE Journals, March 1, 2002, https://journals.sagepub.com/doi/abs/10.1177/0146167202286008

- *"Another research journal article titled, "Flawed Self-Assessment: Implications for Health, Education, and the Workplace," described…"* - David Dunning, SAGE Journals, December 1, 2004, https://journals.sagepub.com/doi/full/10.1111/j.1529-1006.2004.00018.x

Chapter 1: Solving Problems 101 - It's Simple, But Difficult for Most

- *"There's a time in Justin Wren's life that's particularly dark in Chapter 9 of his book, Fight for the Forgotten..." -* Justin Wren, *Fight for the Forgotten*, September 15, 2015, Pages 71 & 75

- *"...the National Survey of Family Growth that almost 50% of all marriages in the United States end in divorce." -* National Survey of Family Growth, 2015, https://www.apa.org/topics/divorce#:~:text=However%2C%20about%2040%20to%2050,subsequent%20marriages%20is%20even%20higher.

- *"As Malcolm Gladwell discusses in his book, Outliers, Bill Gates had a lot of things go right in his life." -* Malcolm Gladwell, *Outliers*, November 18th, 2008, Pages 50 - 55

CHAPTER 2: Most Don't Care (The Undeniable Reality)

- *"The main issues involve the overall increased temperature of the Earth…" -* NASA.gov, https://climate.nasa.gov/solutions/adaptation-mitigation/#:~:text=Key%20Points,pipeline%20(%E2%80%9Cadaptation%E2%80%9D).

- *"Their combined research showed, "there's a more than 95 percent probability that human activities over the past 50 years have warmed our planet."" -* The Intergovernmental Panel of Climate Change, 2018, https://report.ipcc.ch/sr15/pdf/sr15_spm_final.pdf

- *"In the age of instant, we think success suddenly happens to the lucky few who find their way to abundance."* - Tim Redmond, *Power to Create*, November 29, 2011, Page 130

- *"In a world of more than seven billion people, each of us is a drop in the bucket. But with enough drops, we can fill any bucket."* - David Suzuki, The David Suzuki Foundation, https://davidsuzuki.org/story/people-just-like-you-are-inspiring-positive-change/

- *"Here are some simple suggestions that lower your energy consumption, a major factor in the pollution of our environment (provided by the David Suzuki Foundation)."* - The David Suzuki Foundation, https://davidsuzuki.org/what-you-can-do/top-10-ways-can-stop-climate-change/

- *"The World Bank tells us that, "since 1990, the world has reduced the number of people who live in extreme poverty by over half."* - World Bank, October 2016, https://www.freedomfromhunger.org/world-hunger-facts

- *'You'll find on Forbes and other websites this statistic: "Only 8% of people keep their New Year's Resolutions."'* - Dan Diamond, *Forbes*, January 1, 2013, https://www.forbes.com/sites/dandiamond/2013/01/01/just-8-of-people-achieve-their-new-years-resolutions-heres-how-they-did-it/#5ae277d9596b

- *"According to a 2015 study from the US Chamber of Commerce, "75% of employees steal from the workplace and that most do so repeatedly."'* - Ivy Walker, *Forbes*, December 28, 2018, https://www.forbes.com/sites/ivywalker/2018/12/28/your-employees-are-probably-stealing-from-you-here-are-five-ways-to-put-an-end-to-it/#64e000c53386

- *"A typical organization loses 5% of its annual revenues due to employee fraud."* - Rich Russakoff and Mary Goodman, CBS News, July 14, 2011, https://www.cbsnews.com/news/employee-theft-are-you-blind-to-it/

- *"The U.S. Chamber of Commerce estimates that theft by employees costs American companies $20 billion to $40 billion a year."* - INC. Editorial Magazine, May 15, 1999, https://www.inc.com/articles/1999/05/13731.html#:~:text=The%20U.S%20Chamber%20of%20Commerce,more%20than%20%24400%20per%20year.

- *"...participants whose phones sat on their desk performed nearly 20% worse."* - Ron Friedman, Psychology Today, January 6, 2015, https://www.psychologytoday.com/us/blog/glue/201501/is-your-smartphone-making-you-dumb

- *"The Bureau of Labor Statistics shared that workers only work for approximately two hours and 53 minutes."* - Melanie Curtin, Inc. Magazine, July 21, 2016, https://www.inc.com/melanie-curtin/in-an-8-hour-day-the-average-worker-is-productive-for-this-many-hours.html

- *"The Harvard School of Education found that over 50% of the 18-24 year-old Americans surveyed by National Geographic couldn't find the state of New York on a map."* - Clay Clark, The Thrivetime Show, https://www.thrivetimeshow.com/does-it-work/group-interview/

- *"Newsweek revealed that a quarter of employees who use the internet during work watch porn."* - Anna Kuchment, Newsweek, November 28, 2008, https://www.newsweek.com/report-more-employees-visiting-porn-sites-work-85229

- *"...1 in 4 women and 1 in 13 men were sexually abused before the age of 18."* - Centers for Disease Control and Prevention, 2015, https://www.cdc.gov/injury/features/sexual-violence/index.html

- *"According to reports published by the ADA National Network in 2018..."* - Mental Health Fact Sheet, ADA National Network, 2018, https://adata.org/factsheet/health

- *"According to research conducted by the U.S. Census Bureau, nearly 24 million children in America (1 out of 3) live in homes where the biological father is absent."* - U.S. Census Bureau, National Fatherhood Initiative, 2017, https://www.fatherhood.org/the-father-absence-crisis-in-america

- *"...the College Board now shows that just 40% of the high school seniors met benchmarks for college success on average."* - The Condition of College and Career Readiness Report, ACT.org, 2018, https://www.act.org/content/dam/act/unsecured/documents/cccr2018/National-CCCR-2018.pdf

- *"According to a 2018 Gallup poll, 53% of employees are "not engaged" in the workplace."* - Jim Harter, GALLUP, August 26, 2018, https://news.gallup.com/poll/241649/employee-engagement-rise.aspx

- *"...toddlers experience Schadenfreude, the pleasure at another person's distress."* - Tiffany Watt Smith, Lit Hub, November 21, 2018, https://lithub.com/not-just-a-german-word-a-brief-history-of-schadenfreude/

- *"As early as five years old, we view out-group faces as less human than in-group faces."* - Dr. Peter Hills, American

Psychological Association, March 8, 2019, https://www.apa.org/pubs/highlights/peeps/issue-117

- ***"We're Ready to Blame Others for Our Faults."*** - Elizabeth Lozano, PLOS ONE, March 7, 2019, https://www.ncbi.nlm.nih.gov/pmc/articles/PMC6405044/

- ***"We Don't Like Thinking...Or, At Least, Men Don't."*** - Nadia Whitehead, Science Mag, July 3, 2014, https://www.sciencemag.org/news/2014/07/people-would-rather-be-electrically-shocked-left-alone-their-thoughts

- ***"The study defines this as 'moral hypocrisy,' 'a phenomenon in which individuals judge their own transgressions to be less morally objectionable than the same transgressions enacted by others.'"*** - Piercarlo Valdesolo, ELSEVIER Journal of Experimental Social Psychology, September 2008, https://www.sciencedirect.com/science/article/abs/pii/S0022103108000553

- ***"We Become More Disconnected as We Gain Stature."*** - Lou Solomon, Harvard Business Review: Empathy, 2017, Page 64

- ***"We found that people who have endured challenges in the past (like divorce or being skipped over for a promotion) were less likely to show compassion for someone facing the same struggle…"*** - Rachel Ruttan, Harvard Business Review: Empathy, 2017, Page 54

Chapter 3: Trust: The First Dysfunction

- *"To help lay the foundation for our chapter, let's turn to an excerpt from Five Dysfunctions of a Team on how Kathryn sets the tone for this first dysfunction:"* - Patrick Lencioni, *The Five Dysfunctions of a Team*, 2002, Page 43

- *"Only 1/3rd of Americans trust each other."* - Connie Cass, USA Today, November 3, 2013, https://www.usatoday.com/story/news/nation/2013/11/30/poll-americans-dont-trust-one-another/3792179/

- *"Pew Research shared their research on this very topic: "Around three-quarters (73%) of U.S. adults under 30 believe people 'just look out for themselves' most of the time."'* - John Gramlich, Pew Research, August 6, 2019, https://www.pewresearch.org/fact-tank/2019/08/06/young-americans-are-less-trusting-of-other-people-and-key-institutions-than-their-elders/

- *"Pew also reported that "71% [of surveyors] think interpersonal confidence has worsened in the past 20 years."* - Lee Rainie, Pew Research, July 22, 2019, https://www.pewresearch.org/politics/2019/07/22/the-state-of-personal-trust/

- *"Gallup poll research has shown a decline from 70% church attendance in 1999 to 50% church attendance in 2018."* - Jeffrey Jones, GALLUP, April 18, 2019, https://news.gallup.com/poll/248837/church-membership-down-sharply-past-two-decades.aspx

- *"Do you realize the President of the United States has never had a higher average voter approval rating than 70%?"* - FiveThirtyEight, https://projects.fivethirtyeight.com/trump-approval-ratings/

- *"As Joe Rogan interviewed Glenn on the Joe Rogan Experience, he's perplexed by Glenn's whole idea of living in the wild."* - Joe Rogan, The Joe Rogan Experience, December 7, 2019, https://youtu.be/PNocQzhPyac

- *"Pew Research even found that, 'Nearly two-thirds (64%) say that low trust in the federal government makes it harder to solve many of the country's problems.'"* - Lee Rainie and Andrew Perrin, Pew Research, July 22, 2019, https://www.pewresearch.org/fact-tank/2019/07/22/key-findings-about-americans-declining-trust-in-government-and-each-other/

- *"After her rousing speech about the importance of trust, she received initial pushback."* - Patrick Lencioni, *The Five Dysfunctions of a Team*, 2002, Page 45 - 48

- *"The art of transforming a group of young, ambitious individuals into an integrated championship team is not a mechanistic process. It's a mysterious juggling act..."* - Hugh Delehanty and Phil Jackson, *Eleven Rings: The Soul of Success*, May 21, 2013, Page 10

- *'Kathryn levels with them, "I'd trade that false kind of harmony any day for a team's willingness to argue effectively about an issue and then walk away with no collateral damage."'* - Patrick Lencioni, *The Five Dysfunctions of a Team*, 2002, Page 92

- *"For the rest of the day they launched into some of the most passionate debates Joseph had ever heard..."* - Patrick Lencioni, *The Five Dysfunctions of a Team*, 2002, Page 180 & 181

- *"In Jackson's famous "Triangle" system, the coach shares..."* - Hugh Delehanty and Phil Jackson, *Eleven Rings: The Soul of Success*, May 21, 2013, Page 15

- *"70% of employees do not like where they work."* - Carmine Gallo, *Forbes*, November 11, 2011, https://www.forbes.com/sites/carminegallo/2011/11/11/your-emotionally-disconnected-employees/#3453d0db42d5

- *"...over half of Americans can't cover a surprise $500 expense."* - Aimee Picchi, CBS News, January 12, 2017, https://www.cbsnews.com/news/most-americans-cant-afford-a-500-emergency-expense/

CHAPTER 4: THE ENORMOUS PROBLEM WITH SAVING THE WORLD

- *"His command was to, "Raise up your students to hear My voice, to go where My light is dim…"* - Oral Roberts, Oral Roberts University, https://oru.edu/about-oru/vision-mission.php

- *"Andrew Carnegie was the steel magnate in the late 1800s, and was considered one of America's wealthiest individuals."* - Wikipedia, https://en.wikipedia.org/wiki/Andrew_Carnegie

- *"This, then, is held to be the duty of the man of wealth: To set an example of modest, unostentatious living…"* - Andrew Carnegie, *Gospel of Wealth*, June 1889, Page 20

- *"The average 29-year-old did not graduate from a four-year university, but she did start college; held several jobs, including more than two in the last three years…"* - Derek Thompson, The Atlantic, April 20, 2016, https://www.theatlantic.com/business/archive/2016/04/the-average-29-year-old/479139/

- *"…the Bill & Melinda Gates Foundation, making total grant payments of $50 billion over the lifetime of the foundation."* - Foundation Fact Sheet, Bill & Melinda Gates Foundation, https://www.gatesfoundation.org/Who-We-Are/General-Information/Foundation-Factsheet

- *"In study after study, of composers, basketball players, fiction writers, ice skaters, concert pianists…"* - Malcolm Gladwell (quoting Daniel Levitin), *Outliers*, November 18th, 2008, Page 40

Chapter 5: Obsession is Weird

- *"…only 29% of Americans would consider themselves to be savvy with their money."* - Alicia Adamczyk, CNBC News, November 15, 2019, https://www.cnbc.com/2019/11/15/29-percent-of-americans-are-financially-healthy.html

- *"85% of people lie on their resumes..."* - J.T. O'Donnell, Inc. Magazine, August 15, 2017, https://www.inc.com/jt-odonnell/staggering-85-of-job-applicants-lying-on-resumes-.html

- *"...81% of people lie during the job interview."* - Ron Friedman (quoted by HEC Paris), November 15, 2019, https://www.hec.edu/en/news-room/81-people-lie-during-their-job-interviews

Chapter 6: Environment and the Mentorship Gap

- *"Foolish - having or showing a lack of good sense, judgment, or discretion"* - Online Merriam-Webster Dictionary, https://www.merriam-webster.com/dictionary/foolish

- *"They named Florida State the biggest party school in the country and guess who they named as the biggest partier in the country? That's right, Bert Kreischer."* - Eric Hedegaard, Rolling Stones Magazine, April 17, 1997, https://www.rollingstone.com/culture/culture-features/bert-kreischer-the-undergraduate-240847/

- *"The #2 highest grossing comedy film currently is Hangover Part II..."* - Liz Flynn, Money Inc, September 2019, https://moneyinc.com/top-grossing-comedy-movies-of-all-time/

- *"In the first "Sober October" podcast with Joe Rogan, Ari Shaffir and Tom Segura, the crew decided to rally together in a four-hour podcast to put down a bet."* - Joe Rogan, The Joe Rogan Experience, September 4, 2017, https://youtu.be/tjegWo2oPVg

- *"He started back in 2013, uploading his lectures online."* - Joe Rogan, The Joe Rogan Experience, November 28, 2016, https://youtu.be/04wyGK6k6HE

- *"...his teachings on "Slaying the Dragon Within Us," and other religious deep-dives, caught on."* - Dr. Jordan Peterson, Youtube, January 26, 2016, https://youtu.be/REjUkEj1O_0

- *"At one point, during one of his lectures, he's seen on Youtube being massively booed by a mob of students."* - Patricia Marcoccia, "The Rise of Jordan Peterson", September 26, 2019, Netflix (Documentary Title Here: https://www.youtube.com/watch?v=Y3zkvJBXLQg)

- *"Only 16% of the kids in the South Bronx education system perform at or above their appropriate grade level in math."* - Malcolm Gladwell, *Outliers*, November 18th, 2008, Page 260 - 269

Chapter 7: Apathetic vs. Non-Apathetic: A Case Study

- *"Kevin Hart was declared by TIME magazine in 2015, as one of the 100 most influential people in the world."* - Moriba Cummings, BET Network, April 16, 2015, https://www.bet.com/news/celebrities/2015/04/16/kevin-hart-kanye-west-and-laverne-cox-included-in-time-s-100-most-influential-people-list.html

- *"Jim Stovall became an Olympic weightlifting champion, best-selling author, television network creator and multi-millionaire, all AFTER turning blind in his mid-20s."* - Clay Clark, The Thrivetime Show, https://www.thrivetimeshow.com/podcast-guests/jim-stovall/

- *"Sean Stephenson spent 30 years of his life doing motivational speaking in front of millions of people…"* - Clay Clark, The Thrivetime Show, https://www.thrivetimeshow.com/podcast-guests/sean-stephenson/

- *"Shane is a man who's pathetically apathetic. He may be the very definition of this phrase."* - Paul Neilan, *Apathy and Other Small Victories*, May 2, 2006, Pages 146, 147, 159, 195-196

- *"Gretchen Rubin asked a question that everyone has likely asked themselves, 'What do I want from life, anyway?'"* - Gretchen Rubin, *The Happiness Project*, 2009, Page 1, 2, 12-14, 25, 32, 33-34, 40, 288

- *"She graduated with an undergraduate degree and law degree from Yale and became editor-in-chief for the Yale Law Journal."* - Wikipedia, https://en.wikipedia.org/wiki/Gretchen_Rubin

CHAPTER 9: BUT, WAIT...DO YOU REALLY?

- *"...look into Planned Parenthood's website and read about their "Take Action" or "Volunteer" pages."* - Planned Parenthood Action Fund, https://www.istandwithpp.org/take-action, https://www.plannedparenthood.org/get-involved

- *"It turns out that 34 hours of practicing a language on Duolingo equates to a semester-long college course."* - Roumen Vesselinov and John Grego, Doulingo, December 2012, http://static.duolingo.com/s3/DuolingoReport_Final.pdf

- *"In research conducted by Roumen Vesselinov, a research associate at the University of Maryland in Baltimore, he commented to Vice magazine that the jump from novice to advanced is "noteworthy."* - Mike Pearl, VICE Magazine, January 12, 2017, https://www.vice.com/en_us/article/ezxyyz/are-duolingo-users-actually-learning-anything-useful

- *"Or how only 30% of businesses will survive for 10 years?"* - Georgia McIntyre, Fundera, July 22, 2020, https://www.fundera.com/blog/what-percentage-of-small-businesses-fail

- *"Here's the one size fits all excuse for all situations where any area of existence isn't going the way you want it to go…"* - Jim Stovall, The Thrivetime Show, https://www.thrivetimeshow.com/business-podcasts/blind-multi-million-dollar-entrepreneur-jim-stovall-explains-how-to-properly-manage-employees/

- *"Thanks to the consulting firm I work at; they give business owners a great way to break down goals that are important to their lives."* - Clay Clark and Dr. Robert Zoellner, *BOOM: The Business Coach Playbook: The 13 Proven Steps to Business Success*, January 12, 2017, Page 7

Chapter 10: "Be Fruitful, Then Multiply."

- *"What my boss will say is, 'Be fruitful, then multiply.'"* - Tim Redmond, *Power to Create*, November 29, 2011, Pages 127-142

- *"Dr. Jordan Peterson discusses this in 12 Rules for Life. Rule #6 states that we should 'set our house in perfect order before we criticize the world.'"* - Dr. Jordan Peterson, *12 Rules for Life*, January 16, 2018, Page 157

Chapter 11: Daily Planning & Time Blocking

- *"...yet, less than 30% of our US population votes in these local elections."* - Zoltan Hajnal, *New York Times*, October 22, 2018, https://www.nytimes.com/2018/10/22/opinion/why-does-no-one-vote-in-local-elections.html

- *"For a mind-blowing experience, go onto Youtube and search 'Joe Rogan's first podcast episode.'"* - Joe Rogan, The Joe Rogan Experience, January 17, 2013, https://youtu.be/ZWBCnvOuXK8

- *"Only by setting aside specific time in our schedules for traction (the action that draws us toward what we want in life) can we turn our*

- *backs on distraction."* - Nir Eyal, *Indistractable: How to Control Your Attention and Choose Your Life*, August 6, 2019, Page 56

- *"…eliminate all white space on your calendar…"* - Nir Eyal, *Indistractable: How to Control Your Attention and Choose Your Life*, August 6, 2019, Page 56

- *"Adults spend an average of 144 minutes a day on social media alone."* - J. Clement, Statista, February 26, 2020, https://www.statista.com/statistics/433871/daily-social-media-usage-worldwide/

- *"According to Pew Research, 'Roughly half (54%) believe they spend too much time on their cell phone…'"* - Jingjing Jiang, Pew Research, August 22, 2018, https://www.pewresearch.org/internet/2018/08/22/how-teens-and-parents-navigate-screen-time-and-device-distractions/

- *"…46% said they "feel addicted" to their mobile devices."* - James Steyer, Common Sense Media, 2019, https://www.commonsensemedia.org/sites/default/files/uploads/research/2019-new-normal-parents-teens-screens-and-sleep-united-states.pdf

- *"In 2015, the average person received approximately 64 phone notifications per day."* - Martin Pielot and Luz Rello, Pielot Research, 2017, http://pielot.org/pubs/PielotRello2017-MHCI-DoNotDisturb.pdf

- *"Studies have shown that people with their phones in another room "significantly outperformed" those who had their phones on the desk..."* - Adrian Ward, McCombs School of Business: University of Texas, June 26, 2017, https://news.utexas.edu/2017/06/26/the-mere-presence-of-your-smartphone-reduces-brain-power/

- *"Nir Eyal, the best-selling author of the book, Indistractable, shares research from PPAI…"* - Nir Eyal, *Indistractable: How to Control Your Attention and Choose Your Life*, August 6, 2019, Page 54

- *"'Life's too short' is repeated often enough to be a cliché, but this time it's true."* - Seth Godin, *Tribes: We Need You to Lead Us*, April 22, 2014

Chapter 12: What Will You Be Satisfied With?

- *"Living like today is your first day on Earth opens you up to all possibilities..."* - Joshua Bradley, Medium.com blog, July 29, 2017, https://medium.com/@airjoshb/why-living-each-day-like-its-your-last-is-bad-advice-c9ec6787b273

- *"There are even more negative statistics discussing how 'the suicide rate increased 33 percent from 1999 through 2017.'"* - Kirsten Weir, American Psychological Association, March 2019, https://www.apa.org/monitor/2019/03/trends-suicide

- *"Suicide ranks as the fourth leading cause of death for people ages 35 to 54..."* - Kirsten Weir, American Psychological Association, March 2019, https://www.apa.org/monitor/2019/03/trends-suicide

- *"...during his first book, The Power Broker, his wife sold the house without his knowledge to keep food on the table."* - Kirsten Weir, American Psychological Association, March 2019, https://www.apa.org/monitor/2019/03/trends-suicide

www.ingramcontent.com/pod-product-compliance
Lightning Source LLC
Chambersburg PA
CBHW021940290426
44108CB00012B/914